# CRACKING
# THE WINE CODE

By Lavinia Brown

First published by Lavinia Brown, May 2009

Copyright © Lavinia Brown, 2009

www.laviniabrown.co.uk

Typeset, printed and bound in Great Britain by Healeys Print Group, Ipswich

Lavinia Brown is hereby identified as author of this work in accordance with the Copyright, Designs and Patents Act 1988.

978-0-9562549-0-0

CRACKING THE WINE CODE is the starting point for any curious but frustrated wine drinker: someone who doesn't know much about wine other than the fact that they enjoy it, someone who wants to understand why they prefer a particular wine over another and how to recognise one that is similar.

It provides the answers to all your wine queries: a systematic approach to defining your preferences, an explanation of how to make sense of a wine label and a shopping-friendly style guide to the most common grape varieties and wine regions on the market.

It also includes practical tips on serving, storing and buying wine, hints on how you can tell if a wine is off, plus some easy rules to follow when you want to pair wine with a meal. For the budding wine expert there are insights into buying at auction, advice on investing in wine 'futures' and an introduction to how traditional as well as alternative, organic and biodynamic wines are produced.

I hope that this book empowers you with the confidence to experiment – wine should be fun and unpretentious and above all, it should be enjoyed. Happy tasting!

# HOW TO CHOOSE WINE WITH CONFIDENCE

# TOP WINE TIPS

# THE TECHNICAL BIT

# HOW TO CHOOSE WINE WITH CONFIDENCE

## DEFINING YOUR PREFERENCES

*Confidence comes from knowing which styles of wine you enjoy. Do you generally prefer wines that are full-bodied, high in alcohol and bursting with fruit for example, or lighter-bodied, delicately-flavoured, more refreshing styles? To find out, you need to know how to **taste** a wine rather than drink it. This involves breaking down the process of drinking and looking at each part of the sensory experience: at the wine's **appearance**, **smell** and **taste**. By doing so, it becomes easy to establish what you find attractive and why.*

## How to evaluate wine

## APPEARANCE

**COLOUR**

You can judge a wine's maturity by tilting the glass at a 45° angle away from you. As you do this the wine separates into two: the rim, which is the thin watery edge where the wine reaches the glass and the core, which holds the main body of colour. The first signs of age can be seen in the rim: red wines get paler as they mature whereas white wines get darker. Red wines start off a deep purple colour and slowly turn more reddish until they eventually turn brown. White wines begin with an almost greenish tinge and turn gradually more gold until they become amber-coloured. Assessing a wine's colour is useful because if a wine looks more mature than its vintage[1], this may be a sign that it has been badly stored: an environment that is too warm will speed up a wine's ageing process and turn it brown more quickly than is normal.

Wine colour also tells you a bit about its style: a red wine that has a bluish hue is likely to be less acidic than a more reddish example, whereas a golden tinge in a white wine may either indicate the use of oak during its vinification or that its grapes were affected by noble rot[2].

**DENSITY**

A wine's density refers to the intensity of its colour and can be measured by placing the glass on a white surface and looking down through the wine towards the stem. In a red wine, if you are unable to see it then the wine is described as densely-coloured. This means it is the product of very ripe grapes because as these ripen and become sweeter, they also darken in colour. A dense wine is likely to be full-bodied and have a concentrated fruit flavour. A pale wine on the other hand, is likely to be lighter in body and more delicate in flavour with a lower fruit concentration. A densely-coloured red wine would also indicate that it was made from a grape variety with thick skin because red wine grapes are vinified along with their skins (as opposed to white wine grapes whose skins are removed prior to fermentation). The thicker the skin of the red grape and the longer this remains in contact with its juice, the deeper and denser the colour of the resulting wine. A Pinot Noir-based wine is therefore usually less dense and lighter in colour than a Cabernet Sauvignon-based wine because the former's grapes are small, tightly-clustered and relatively thin-skinned in comparison to the latter's large, thick-skinned grapes.

A wine's density should always match the types of grape variety in its blend. If a wine is denser looking than you think is appropriate, this may be because its fruit has been over-extracted and it will taste flabby and lack structure. Likewise paleness in a wine may indicate that its grapes were not very ripe when they were harvested. This could either be because the vintage was 'bad' and the grapes did not receive enough sunshine to ripen sufficiently or because they were grown in a cool climate. Thus a Pinot Noir-based wine produced in the Loire Valley is likely to be less densely-coloured than its more southerly Burgundian or hotter-climate, New World[3] counterpart.

## LEGS / TEARS

Wine legs are the channels that run down the inside of a glass after you swirl the wine to release its aromas. They give an indication of the wine's residual sugar[4] levels and thus an idea of its body and alcohol content. They are most evident in wines that are over 12% alcoholic strength.

Legs are not a sign of quality but are in fact the result of a complex relationship between the rate at which alcohol evaporates from wine, the differing surface tensions of water and alcohol (which are the principle ingredients of a wine) and the 'interfacial tension' between the glass and the wine, which refers to the way in which it grips the side of the glass.

# BOUQUET

A wine's perfume is usually referred to as its bouquet or nose. To assess this you need to swirl the wine to release its aromas and then take a short, sharp sniff. (Repeated, long sniffs will deaden your sense of smell). Its bouquet should give you a general idea of whether you will like its taste because both senses are intimately linked (hence it is often hard to detect flavours when you have a cold).

## CHARACTER

The easiest way to describe a wine's bouquet is to categorise it by type: is its predominant aroma a fruity, floral or spicy one? Or is it nutty, vegetal (can you smell green beans or straw) or earthy (can you detect hints of flint, compost or mushroom)? The most pronounced aroma might instead be a woody one, in which case you would smell sandalwood, coffee or burnt toast aromas; perhaps it is microbiological in type and reminds you of olive brine, cheese or wax; or maybe it is more chemical and you can detect a hint of 'wet dog' or diesel? Categorising a smell by type is not easy because the mind often finds it hard to disassociate an aroma from the object it normally pairs with it; it can therefore seem wrong to smell certain things in a wine. In fact, all sorts of incongruous aromas can be associated with it such as 'wet pavement' (found in some Claret), 'sweaty saddle' (a characteristic of Australian Shiraz), 'tar and roses' (found in Italian Barolo) and even petrol (found in young Riesling). Identifying aromas comes with practise: the wider the range you commit to memory from smelling everyday objects around you, the easier it becomes to recognise them in wine.

You may notice that a wine's bouquet changes over the period of time it is exposed to air. This is because its aromas evaporate over time (which is the reason wines are often decanted - this softens them and encourages their aromas to develop). With increased exposure however, a wine's bouquet will eventually disappear altogether and it will start to turn to vinegar.

## INTENSITY
An intense bouquet is usually an indicator of quality. A weak bouquet on the other hand, is not necessarily a sign of poor quality: it may be the result of the wine's serving temperature, the fact that it has been shaken up or a sign that it is going through a temporary 'closed'[5] phase in its maturity when it smells and tastes bland. (This last phenomenon has still not been explained chemically and is therefore impossible as yet to predict or cure).

## TASTE

Assessing the taste of a wine not only entails evaluating its flavour and intensity but also its structure, which is an umbrella term that includes its body, texture, sweetness, acidity, tannins, alcohol level and length[6]. To assess its flavour, you need to draw air through the wine by slurping, which encourages the release of aromas. Then you need to swirl the wine around the various tasting areas: the tongue, cheeks, gums and the back of your mouth, each of which reacts differently to the factors that make up a wine's structure. If both its structure and flavour are in balance and no particular trait is more obvious than another, the wine can be described as rounded[7] or balanced, which is the ultimate sign of quality.

### CHARACTER

As a general rule: fine wines show a wider range of more complex flavours than simple, everyday-drinking wines. Identifying and describing these flavours however can be quite a challenge, so the easiest way to start is by categorising them by type (as with a wine's bouquet). For example does the wine taste fruity or floral? If it is fruity, which category of fruit does its flavour belong to: citrus, dried or tropical? If it is more tropical-tasting than citrusy, is this flavour closer to the taste of a melon, pineapple or lychee?

By applying this kind of systematic approach to tasting a wine, you can learn to identify particular flavours. Some of these may indicate how the wine was vinified: ageing in oak casks can contribute cinnamon or sandalwood aromas for example and if the wine underwent a secondary malolactic fermentation[8] (MLF), this can add buttery aromas.

## INTENSITY

The intensity of a wine's flavour reveals the ripeness of its grapes when they were picked. It can also indicate whether the grape must (juice) has been concentrated[9]. As long as a wine's flavour concentration and structure seem balanced, a pronounced flavour is usually a sign of quality. A wine that has a pronounced flavour but that is lacking in structure is described as flabby or fat.

## BODY & MOUTHFEEL

In order to gauge whether the body of a wine is light, medium or full, you need to swirl it round your mouth. If it feels thin or one-dimensional, this is usually a sign of poor quality. Body alone however does not make a quality wine. The most important measure of this is that a wine's components are balanced: a lighter-bodied wine should therefore display correspondingly delicate fruit and acidity whereas a full-bodied wine requires concentrated, ripe fruit and a pronounced structure to give an impression of balance.

Alcohol has a higher viscosity (resistance to movement) than water so wines that feel 'heavy' usually have a high alcohol content. Full-bodied wines also indicate that their grapes were ripe when they were harvested so a hot-climate, Australian Shiraz for example is likely to feel heavier than a cool-climate, French Cabernet Franc-based wine from the Loire Valley.

Swirling a wine also gives you a sense of its 'mouthfeel' (texture). This is described with adjectives that usually apply to solids or materials such as silky, waxy, oily or velvety.

**SWEETNESS**

Sweetness is detected by the tip of the tongue. It is therefore one of the first things you notice about a wine and is usually yet another indicator of how ripe the grapes were when they were harvested. This is because a grape's acidity levels decrease and its sugar levels increase as it ripens. During fermentation yeasts convert these natural sugars into alcohol. Most yeasts cannot tolerate alcohol concentrations of over 15% so if there is any sugar left to convert when this level is reached, it is described as residual sugar. Wines from hot-climate countries in which grapes ripen easily have high levels of residual sugar and alcohol and are therefore more likely to taste sweeter than those from cool-climate countries where grapes may struggle to ripen adequately. This is also because ethanol[10] can taste sweet (in concentrations of 13% or higher).

A wine is described as dry if it contains less than 2 grammes per litre of residual sugar. It can also seem dry when its sweetness is masked. This is achieved either by serving it very cold, by the presence of bubbles (in the case of a sparkling wine) or because it has high tannin and acidity levels too (which provide a counterbalance to its sweetness and therefore make it seem less obvious).

**ACIDITY**

A wine's acidity is measured by the watering sensation it produces along the sides of your tongue: the higher the acidity, the more your mouth waters. Acidity is an essential component of a wine because it counterbalances its fruit concentration, sweetness and tannins and makes it taste fresh. Too much acidity means the grapes were not sufficiently ripe when they were picked, either because there was not enough sunshine during their growing season or because the winemaker was forced to harvest them early in order to avoid bad weather. If this occurs, the grape must can be deacidified in the cellar before it is fermented into wine.

Some grape varieties are naturally more acidic than others such as Sauvignon Blanc and Chenin Blanc. These produce wines that seem more crisp and less full-bodied than those made from less acidic varieties such as Chardonnay or Semillon. The level of acidity that is acceptable in a wine depends not only on its grape variety but also on the occasion at which it is served and the food with which it is paired – high acidity is sought-after in white wine aperitifs and in sparkling wines (acidity stimulates the appetite), as well as in red wines to be paired with fatty or rich meat dishes (these are usually too high in acidity to drink alone).

### TANNINS

Tannins are identified by the gums and insides of your cheeks and a wine with high tannin levels will produce an astringent or 'drying' sensation. This occurs when its tannins react with the collagen proteins inside your mouth and turn them into leather (this is also how tanners create leather from animal hide hence the name of the trade). Eating food and in particular protein at the same time as drinking a tannic wine acts as a substitute for the collagen found in your cheeks and gums and thereby mitigates the wine's astringent effect. This is why particularly tannic wines such as Italian Barolo and some Clarets are usually paired with meat or cheese dishes to 'soften' them.

If a wine's tannin levels are too high it will have an unpleasantly astringent effect, like tea that has been steeped for too long. This may either be because the wine is not yet ready for drinking or because the weather was poor that vintage and the grapes did not reach sugar maturity. Aerating or decanting a wine will soften it.

Tannins are primarily found in a grape's skins, seeds and stems so red wines, which are made by keeping these in contact with the must during fermentation have higher tannin levels than rosé or white wines, which spend less or no time in contact with them. Tannins are also imparted by the wooden barrels in which red wines and certain fuller-bodied white wines are aged. The newer the wood of the barrel and the less toast[11] it has received, the more tannic its effect on a wine.

Like acids, tannins prevent a wine tasting flabby and provide a counterbalance to its sweet fruit concentration. They also play a part in allowing a wine's flavours to mature by helping it retain its colour and by delaying its transformation to vinegar. As a wine ages, its tannins slowly precipitate out of solution and gravitate to the bottom of the bottle to form sediment. This is why wines soften and lose colour as they mature.

### ALCOHOL LEVEL & LENGTH

A wine that is produced in the EU must have an alcoholic content of between 8.5% and 15%. Alcohol level is not a reflection of a wine's quality but of the ripeness of the grapes when they were harvested – the riper the grapes and the higher their sugar levels at the time of harvest, the higher the potential alcohol level of the resulting wine. (A wine that has an alcoholic content of 14.5% is therefore not necessarily superior to one that has an alcoholic content of just 10%, merely the product of riper, sweeter grapes).

Alcohol is detected by the back of the mouth, which produces a warming sensation once the wine has either been swallowed or spat out. As a general rule: the greater the warming sensation, the higher the wine's alcohol levels although a high alcohol wine that also has high acidity and high tannin levels will taste balanced rather than 'hot'.

The length of a wine refers to its persistence of flavour and contributes greatly to your overall impression of it. Indeed the French even invented a means of measuring it: a 'caudalie' refers to each second of sensory impact that can be experienced after swallowing or spitting out a wine. As a general rule: the longer a wine's length, the better its quality.

## UMAMI
Umami is acknowledged by the Japanese to be the fifth primary taste. It is caused by the presence of the amino acid glutamate and is found in parmesan cheese, soy sauce, seaweed and tuna. In an attempt to recreate this sensation in other foods, the seasoning monosodium glutamate was developed. The term means both essence and delicious, and gives the taster an impression of either meatiness, savouriness or of rounded 'completeness'. Its presence is said to be affected by the ripeness of the grapes when harvested but because it is hard to define and overlaps the other primary tastes, it can be difficult to identify in a wine.

## Setting up a tasting

The best way to learn how to taste a wine rather than drink it, is to set up your own tasting. You can include various bottles of both red and white wine each of which should ideally represent a different region or grape variety. (Vintage is not quite as important so wines from within the last three or so years will do). By simultaneously comparing the wines and assessing in turn their appearance, smell and lastly taste, you will soon see what makes each unique. (It is far easier to break each wine down rather than compare overall impressions which are easy forgotten once you have moved onto the next wine).

WINES
Four bottles of red and four bottles of white should be enough to establish a sufficient contrast in styles. Depending on how many people attend, you will probably only need one bottle of each (you should be able to get about fifteen 50ml tasting samples from a standard bottle, as opposed to six drinking glasses).

The red wines should be tasted at room temperature and need to have been upright for at least an hour prior to the tasting (this is so that any bitter sediment they might contain will have gravitated to the bottom of the bottle. If you are tasting older vintages, they may even need to be decanted). The white wines on the other hand, should be tasted at a slightly warmer temperature than you would normally drink them so that their aromas are not masked by the cold. (It is the evaporation of aromas that creates a wine's perfume; the cold slows down the rate of evaporation so a wine that is served too cold may seem void of any smell).

## WHERE, WHEN & HOW

So that your senses are not distracted by any outside influences, the tasting should be held in as neutral an environment as possible: the room should be light enough to describe the wine's colour and density, and should neither smell of food, smoke, flowers nor perfume. The ideal time to compare wines is in the morning when your taste buds are at their most alert (although beware of using strong toothpaste just beforehand)! Failing this, before or after, rather than with a meal is best. This is because your impression of a wine can be adversely affected or enhanced by different types of food and you want to be judging the wines as objectively as possible as well as on their own merits. Your impression can also be influenced by the order in which you taste so the wines should be grouped together by colour: sparkling first, then white, rosé, red and lastly sweet wines. They should be grouped according to their body too: light, fruity ones should be tasted first, followed by the more weighty, structured wines. (If you are not sure how to place them in order, a description of each wine's style is often found on its back label). Plain crackers are a good way to cleanse your palate in between examples.

## GLASSWARE

For tasting as opposed to drinking wine, a tulip-shaped glass is best. This allows a wine's aromas to concentrate at the rim of the glass, which makes it easier to describe the wine's perfume. The glasses should be spotlessly clean because dust or leftover detergent smells can interfere with the smell and taste of a wine. You should pour only a third of a glass of each wine per person – this minimises the risk of spillage when you swirl the wine to release its flavours. In order to differentiate between the wines you can use coloured stickers placed on each glass and a tasting sheet (see example).

# TASTING SHEET

| | |
|---|---|
| Wine Name & Producer | Jackson Estate, Sauvignon Blanc |
| Provenance (Country and Region) | Marlborough, New Zealand |
| Vintage & Alcohol | 2006, 12.5% |
| Price | £11.07 |
| Tasting Date & Circumstances | April 1st 08, dinner with friends (grilled sole) |

## APPEARANCE:

| | |
|---|---|
| Colour | clear, pale, straw colour; big watery rim |
| Density | – |
| Faults? | – |

## BOUQUET:

| | |
|---|---|
| Character | very fresh and clean – grassy, herbaceous (nettles), slight hint of gooseberry? |
| Intensity | medium pronounced |
| Faults? [12] | – |

## TASTE:

| | |
|---|---|
| Character | slightly honeyed flavour at first, develops into sweetish gooseberry fruit; lemon finish |
| Intensity | pronounced flavour, more intense on the palate than on the nose |
| Body & Mouthfeel | medium body, quite silky, feels very clean |
| Sweetness | – |
| Acidity | very high, crisp acidity; sharp, clean finish |
| Tannins | – |
| Alcohol Level & Length | medium alcohol – good balance overall, very good candied lemon length |
| Faults? | |

## OVERALL IMPRESSION:

| | |
|---|---|
| Varietal Correctness [13] | pleasantly Old World in style (high acidity and quite elegant) reminded me of a Muscadet? |
| Value for Money | great wine but bit expensive. Good for an 'occasion'... |
| Personal Evaluation | packed with flavour and yet a very elegant wine, nicely balanced. Really enjoyed it. Lovely with food (in particular fish without a sauce, maybe even a chicken salad?), would be good by itself too. Might try a younger vintage next time as this one has a bit of bottle age? Would buy again! |

## Major global grape varieties [14]

Now that you can describe the types of wines you generally prefer, it is good to be familiar with the styles and flavours of wines produced by the most common grape varieties and wine regions of the world. This way you can make an educated guess as to whether you will like them or not.

There are over a thousand different grape varieties suitable for making wine. Most of these can be found growing somewhere in the world but only a small minority are both widely-planted and internationally-recognised. The most important are called 'noble' grape varieties because they are sufficiently dependable to produce high quality wines in various locations without being too demanding about the conditions in which they are grown. Many are now household names such as Chardonnay, Sauvignon Blanc, Cabernet Sauvignon and Merlot.

# WHITE

## CHARDONNAY

Chardonnay is one of the world's most widely-planted grape varieties and varies greatly in style depending upon where it is grown and how it is vinified. Indeed in response to New World winemakers' over-zealous fruit extraction and heavy-handed use of oak during its vinification in the 1990s, the grape suffered in popularity and there was a consumer backlash towards it summarised in the phrase ABC or 'anything-but-Chardonnay'.

STYLE & FLAVOUR:
*Hot Climate examples*[15]: rounded wines that are full-bodied with a lowish acidity and display buttery, tropical or tinned-fruit flavours of peach, pineapple and lychee.
*Cool Climate examples*: elegant, complex wines with medium acidity levels, a rounded, full body and lots of finesse. These are less buttery than their hot-climate counterparts and display fresh fruit flavours of pear and apple as well as toasty or nutty aromas.

WHERE IT COMES FROM[16]:
Chardonnay is epitomised by its most elegant (and probably expensive) expression in the fine white wines from the Côte d'Or[17] region of Burgundy. It produces characteristically lean, steely examples in Chablis, fuller-bodied, less complex versions in southern Burgundy (such as Mâcon, Rully, St. Véran and Pouilly Fuissé) and easy-drinking wines in the South of France (particularly in the form of inexpensive Vin de Pays). Among other places, it is also planted in Switzerland and Spain (Catalonia), Australia (Margaret River, Upper Hunter Valley),

Tasmania (where it produces a cool-climate style wine), California (Sonoma and Napa Valleys), America (Washington and Oregon produce delicious cool-climate styles) and New Zealand (Hawke's Bay, Marlborough and Martinborough).

**WHAT IT GOES WITH:**
Most Chardonnays suit every occasion (even pairing with white meat dishes or cold cuts). Lighter to medium-bodied Old World[18] versions (Chablis and Vin de Pays) are best without food (they can be too weak to stand up to particularly rich dishes) as are full-bodied New World versions, which can overpower certain dishes with their buttery aromas. The ultimate food partner is a Burgundian Chardonnay from the Côte d'Or, which combines a pronounced flavour with a refreshing, elegant structure.

## SAUVIGNON BLANC

**STYLE & FLAVOUR:**
Sauvignon Blanc is generally only grown in cool-climate regions and produces refreshingly crisp, lean to medium-bodied wines with medium to high acidity levels. It is characterised by its fresh, green, grassy aromas and flavours of apple, gooseberry, asparagus and sweet corn.

**WHERE IT COMES FROM:**
This is a key grape in France's Loire Valley where it produces the varietal wines Pouilly-Fumé, Sancerre and the great-value alternative, Quincy. Sauvignon Blanc wines vary in body and roundness depending on how ripe the grapes are at the time of harvest. The vintage and producer of the wine are therefore

important, as is the aspect[19] of the vineyard in which the grapes are grown. This grape is equally synonymous with the wine it produces in New Zealand, which is typically fuller-bodied and more tropically fruit-flavoured than its French counterpart but nonetheless distinguished by its distinctive grassy aroma.

**WHAT IT GOES WITH:**
Sauvignon Blanc is reasonably adaptable but not universally-suited to all foods because of its distinctive herbaceous flavour. It is delicious with light salads, cold or simply-prepared, grilled fish dishes and also with cold cuts. It makes an ideal summer or aperitif wine because of its refreshing zest.

## PINOT GRIGIO (ITALY) / PINOT GRIS (FRANCE) RULÄNDER (GERMANY)

Pinot Grigio is best-known in its Italian or French guise, even though it is more widely-planted in Germany than in France. It is a popular house wine in restaurants and bars.

**STYLE & FLAVOUR:**
This grape produces medium to full-bodied wines with lowish acidity and a distinctive silky or waxy texture. Most examples are mildly aromatic with spicy or grapey fruit flavours; lesser-quality examples are light-bodied and can be bland.

**WHERE IT COMES FROM:**
Pinot Grigio is widely grown in Italy (particularly in the north east): it produces its best examples in the Friuli and Alto Adige regions and its most bland in the Veneto. It is also commonly

found in Switzerland and in the Germanic-French region of Alsace where it produces richly-perfumed, full-bodied almost 'thick' wines which have a peachy, honeyed flavour. It is now gaining favour in the New World too: it is the second most planted variety in California, the most planted variety in Oregon, and is increasingly widespread in New Zealand and Australia.

**WHAT IT GOES WITH:**
Pleasantly easy-to-drink by itself, the most common styles of Pinot Gris are neither too structured nor pronounced in flavour and therefore provide good partners to a range of foods, in particular aromatic, spicy Asian dishes. Rich, full-bodied styles make good partners to the rich dishes of their regions such as Swiss rösti, sausages, grilled cheese and stews.

---

# PINOT BIANCO (ITALY) / PINOT BLANC (FRANCE) WEISSBURGUNDER (GERMANY)

**STYLE & FLAVOUR:**
This grape is generally only grown in cool climates. It is similar in style to an Old World Chardonnay but has higher acidity. It is often vinified in a way that creates a refreshing, slightly sprizty wine with deliberately-induced residual carbon dioxide.

**WHERE IT COMES FROM:**
Pinot Bianco is grown on a small scale in California, Alsace, northern Italy, Germany and Austria (where it makes particularly fine, sweet dessert wines).

**WHAT IT GOES WITH:**
Its wines are as versatile as those of the Chardonnay grape but lack their elegance: they make good partners to a wide range of foods but are perhaps too bland to enhance any in particular which makes them good, light aperitif wines.

# CHENIN BLANC

Because of its particularly high acidity levels, Chenin Blanc is arguably the world's most versatile grape variety and is capable of producing quality sparkling, dry and long-lived sweet white wines.

**STYLE & FLAVOUR:**
*Hot Climate examples*: wines that are refreshingly high in acidity with a fullish body and apricot and melon fruit flavours.
*Cool Climate examples*: medium to full-bodied wines with honeyed, slightly floral aromas and high acidity.

**WHERE IT COMES FROM:**
This grape is widely planted throughout the Loire Valley. Here it produces a range of styles including excellent dessert wines that are on a par with the very best Sauternes but without their price tag (notable examples are Côteaux du Layon, Bonnezeaux and Quarts de Chaume). It is considered more of an everyday-drinking wine grape in South Africa (where it is also called Steen) and is grown in California, South America and Australia too (where it is mostly a blending grape).

**WHAT IT GOES WITH:**
Chenin Blanc produced in a dry style is an easy wine to pair with a range of foods. Old World examples may be more suitable for drinking without food as they are usually vinified to a higher standard and are therefore more complex than those produced in the New World.

---

## RIESLING

Riesling used to be quite rare outside Germany but is now gaining in popularity in the New World. This is justly so, as it is capable of producing very fine wines that continue to improve with age. Many German Riesling wines are off-dry (slightly sweet) so it is important to check this if ordering them in a restaurant.

**STYLE & FLAVOUR:**
*Hot Climate examples*: rounded, medium bodied wines with mineral, peachy apricot flavours and refreshing acidity. New World styles resemble mature Old World examples but lack their elegance.
*Cool Climate examples*: wines that are usually low in alcohol and light to medium-bodied with medium to high acidity. They have a silky texture and a pronounced floral flavour with distinctive minerally or petrol-like aromas when young. These develop into honeyed apricot and peach flavours as the wine matures.

**WHERE IT COMES FROM:**
Germany, Austria, France (Alsace), Australia, New Zealand, California, South Africa and America (Ontario).

**WHAT IT GOES WITH:**
A young, Old World Riesling can be difficult to pair with food because of its pronounced petrol aroma although this, alongside its high acidity, provides the perfect complement to Asian cuisine. When mature its rich, honeyed flavours enhance fish, white-meat or cream-based dishes. New World styles make delicious aperitifs or accompaniments to summer salads.

## GEWÜRZTRAMINER

A niche grape variety that tends to provoke a love or hate reaction because of its very pronounced floral aromas. It is increasingly gaining favour in parts of the New World.

**STYLE & FLAVOUR:**
Gewürztraminer produces medium to full-bodied wines that have a very soft, silky texture and highly-pronounced spicy and floral aromas with hints of rose petals and grapefruit. New World examples display more tropical-fruit flavours such as lychee.

**WHERE IT COMES FROM:**
Alsace, Germany and Eastern Europe, Chile, Australia, New Zealand and California.

**WHAT IT GOES WITH:**
This is probably the least versatile grape variety in terms of food pairing although it makes a superb partner to most Asian cuisine including the rich, highly-flavoured, spicy foods of India and Thailand. (Its acidity provides a refreshing counterbalance to the fat content of the food and its pronounced floral flavours complement most Asian spices). It is best enjoyed very chilled.

# VIOGNIER

Viognier is fairly rare as a varietal[20] wine in the Old World and is best known as a blending element. It became fashionable as a result of the ABC phase and is now planted both in the New World and in the South of France. It generally produces good value, everyday-drinking wines.

**STYLE & FLAVOUR:**
*Hot Climate examples:* rich, alcoholic, full-bodied wines that are decadently-perfumed. These can sometimes seem flabby and lacking in acidity if the grapes are overripe when harvested.
*Cool Climate examples:* produces rounded wines that have a relatively deep yellow colour, medium to high alcohol levels and an almost waxy mouthfeel. They are low to medium in acidity and aromatic with peachy apricot flavours and hints of blossom.

**WHERE IT COMES FROM:**
France (Rhône Valley, Languedoc and the South of France's Vin de Pays), Italy, Austria, South Africa, California, Australia and Chile.

**WHAT IT GOES WITH:**
Viognier is a great everyday-drinking wine and can be enjoyed without food. It also makes a good partner to light or even white-meat dishes that require a full-bodied, rich perfume (such as Christmas turkey). Best enjoyed young and slightly chilled.

# RED

## CABERNET SAUVIGNON

Cabernet Sauvignon is one of the most planted grape varieties in the world and is grown to produce either a varietal wine or the predominant part of a Bordeaux blend.

STYLE & FLAVOUR:
*Hot Climate examples*: rounded, full-bodied wines with medium to high alcohol levels, spicy berry fruit flavours and hints of herbal eucalyptus or mint aromas (especially when produced in Australia).
*Cool Climate examples*: medium-bodied wines that have medium acidity and medium to high tannin and alcohol levels. They display pronounced blackcurrant, smoked meat and leather flavours that are enhanced if they are vinified in oak. These wines are best enjoyed either after a few years' ageing or after an hour or so in a decanter (both encourage their tannins to soften). The finest wines will continue to improve over decades.

WHERE IT COMES FROM:
France (in particular Bordeaux's left-bank[21] where it is the principal ingredient in the finest wines of the region), Eastern Europe, Spain, South America (in particular Chile), Australia and California (both of which produce superbly elegant, ripe-fruit Bordeaux-style wines as well as some over-concentrated, everyday-drinking versions).

WHAT IT GOES WITH:
Old world examples are usually too tannic to be enjoyed without

food but make superb partners to roasted-meat dishes, particularly beef in all forms, pies and stews. New World examples match most meat dishes.

---

# MERLOT

This grape is widely planted around the world and is grown to produce either part of a Bordeaux blend or to make an easy-drinking varietal wine.

**STYLE & FLAVOUR:**
Merlot-based wines are characterised in particular by their very soft, velvety mouthfeel. They are generally fleshy with medium acidity and have low to medium tannins. They show primarily plum-fruit aromas which are accompanied by a hint of herbaceousness if the grapes are not sufficiently ripe when harvested.

**WHERE IT COMES FROM:**
France (in particular Bordeaux's right-bank[22] and its premium 'microchâteaux'[23] wines plus the South of France's Vin de Pays), northern Italy, Eastern Europe, South America (in particular Chile), America (in particular Washington), California and New Zealand.

**WHAT IT GOES WITH:**
This grape is versatile and easy to pair with a range of foods because of its soft tannins and fruity flavour. It makes a good partner to both white and red-meat dishes and even to certain types of chunky white fish such as cod, halibut or monkfish. It is also soft enough to drink alone.

## PINOT NOIR (FRANCE)
## SPÄTBURGUNDER (GERMANY)

This is one of the greatest of all French grapes, epitomised by its expression as a fine red Burgundy. It is now increasingly popular as a varietal wine in the New World despite being rather demanding in terms of its ideal growing conditions. Pinot Noir also produces a small amount of still and sparkling, fruity rosé wine and is one of the main blending ingredients in champagne too.

**STYLE & FLAVOUR:**
Pinot Noir wines are low in tannins and high in acidity and have a characteristically silky texture. Vintage variation is important particularly with Old World examples, which tend to be more elegant and complex than their New World counterparts. In a good vintage when its grapes ripen sufficiently, they produce intensely-perfumed wines with almost caramelised summer-fruit aromas. Under-ripe grapes on the other hand, produce wines that are thin, overly acidic and lacking in fruit. Because of its high acidity, Pinot Noir is capable of continuing to improve after a lengthy ageing period and mature wines display pronounced vegetal, compost-like aromas. Most wines improve with half an hour or so in a decanter, which softens their acidity levels and allows their perfume to develop.

**WHERE IT COMES FROM:**
France (Burgundy, Loire Valley), Switzerland, Germany, Austria, California (in particular Sonoma Valley), Tasmania, New Zealand, America (Oregon and Ontario) and Australia (Yarra Valley, Adelaide Hills).

**WHAT IT GOES WITH:**
The versatility of Pinot Noir wines depends upon their
provenance and age: New World examples are delicious with or
without food and make great partners to white and red-meat
dishes as well as to most fish; Old World examples may be
slightly too acidic to enjoy without food but make superb
partners to lamb and pork. The vegetal aromas produced by
mature wines provide the perfect complement to game. Pinot
Noir also provides a good red wine partner to Asian cuisine.

# SHIRAZ (AUSTRALIA) / SYRAH (FRANCE)

This grape is most famous in its guise either as a big, blockbuster
Australian Shiraz or as the principal ingredient of the Rhône
Valley's finest wines.

**STYLE & FLAVOUR:**
*Hot Climate examples*: densely-coloured, rich and full-bodied wines
which have a high alcohol content, medium to high tannins and
medium acidity. Most are characterised by a peppery,
blackcurrant flavour that has an almost vegetal quality described
in Australia as resembling 'sweaty saddle'. Shiraz is frequently
blended with Cabernet Sauvignon to produce big, fruity
everyday-drinking wines and is popular in Australia as an
unusual sparkling wine to be enjoyed at Christmas.
*Cool Climate examples*: produces hedonistically-perfumed, very
elegant wines which have a silky texture, a characteristic spiciness
and blackcurrant and mulberry fruit flavours. Syrah wines tend to
be medium to high in alcohol content with medium acidity and
tannins. The finest wines continue to improve with age.

**WHERE IT COMES FROM:**
France (Northern Rhône Valley's Côte Rôtie and Hermitage regions, Southern Rhône's Châteauneuf-du-Pape region, South of France), Australia (in particular NSW), South Africa and Argentina.

**WHAT IT GOES WITH:**
The fullest Australian Shiraz wines should only be paired with dishes that are sufficiently powerful in flavour to stand up to them such as spicy, char-grilled or barbecued meats and sausages. Old World examples tend to be more elegant and less full-bodied than this and their spicy character complements roasted meats, in particular game and lamb, pies and stews. Most Syrah wines can be enjoyed without food because of their soft tannins but nonetheless benefit from three quarters of an hour or so in a decanter before drinking so that their aromas have time to develop.

## Lesser global grape varieties [24]

In addition to the world's major global grape varieties there are also other lesser-known, up-and-coming varieties. These may not be considered quite noble enough to produce varietal wines wherever they are grown, but they excel in some climates and in others form reliable parts of a blend, contributing either structure, colour or alcohol to it. Together, both groups of grapes form the basis of most commercially-available, internationally-exported wines.

## WHITE

## COLOMBARD

Colombard was popular in California in the 1980s and 1990s and produces unexciting but pleasant, everyday-drinking, refreshing white wines. It is more likely nowadays to be part of a New World or southern French Chardonnay or Chenin Blanc-based blend, to which it adds acidity.

## SEMILLON

Most commonly vinified as part of a blend (often alongside Sauvignon Blanc), Semillon adds body and texture to a wine. Almost all still white Bordeaux wines are a result of this combination including the dessert wine Sauternes (which is made using only those Semillon grapes which have been affected by noble rot, or 'la pourriture noble'). It is also popular in Australia, particularly in the Hunter Valley.

## VERDELHO

Verdelho is a relatively rare varietal wine grape that is more commonly grown to produce Madeira. It is also vinified in Australia where it produces an everyday-drinking, soft, full-bodied and fruity wine.

# RED

## CABERNET FRANC

Cabernet Franc usually forms part of a blend alongside Shiraz (particularly in Australia), Cabernet Sauvignon or Merlot grapes. It is one of the dominant grape varieties in Bordeaux's right-bank St. Emilion and Pomerol wines, and produces very elegant varietal examples in the Loire Valley's Saumur-Champigny region as well as slightly more rustic versions in its Chinon region. Its wines are medium-bodied and medium in acidity and are defined by their refreshingly stalky, redcurrant and green pepper aromas. Their quality is very dependent upon vintage and in less good years they can seem acidic and woody if the grapes do not ripen sufficiently. Cabernet Franc-based wines are a good match to red meat dishes and may even be enjoyed slightly chilled with cold cuts.

## GRENACHE (FRANCE) / GARNACHA (SPAIN) CANNONAU (ITALY)

This grape produces easy-drinking, soft but reasonably alcoholic wines with pronounced raspberry fruit flavours and a hint of 'road tar'. Grenache is vinified as an everyday-drinking varietal wine in the South of France and California but also makes a potent rosé wine in the Rhône Valley. Tavel is a particularly alcoholic, full-bodied example that is reputedly the best rosé wine in France. The grape is widely-planted in Spain and forms a major part of both its Rioja and Priorat wines. Alongside the Syrah grape, it is also one of the dominant ingredients in France's

Châteauneuf-du-Pape blends. In Italy's most southern regions (especially Sardinia) it produces an intense, full-flavoured almost spicy wine with leather, morello-cherry and caramel aromas. It is an easy grape to pair with most meat dishes but tends to fade when decanted.

## MALBEC

Malbec is grown as a blending grape in Bordeaux as well as in southern France where it forms the backbone of its inky and intense Cahors wine. It is probably better-known however in its Argentinean guise, where it produces full-bodied and dense wines that have a ripe, fleshy softness reminiscent of the finest Pomerols. These wines have lengthy ageing potential and high alcohol levels and are deliciously concentrated with spicy fruit and tobacco flavours. The finest examples benefit from at least half an hour in a decanter so that their aromas can develop. New World Malbec (it is now also grown in Chile) can be enjoyed by itself or with roast red meat dishes or game. Cahors is best partnered with the equally rich dishes of the region such as roast duck or cassoulet.

## SANGIOVESE

This is the principal grape variety grown in many Italian wine regions where it is capable of producing great wines with slightly floral aromas. It is the main grape in a Chianti blend and the sole grape variety in Brunello di Montalcino. It varies greatly in quality according to its winemaker and vintage because it is naturally high in acidity and tannins and therefore requires ripe fruit to flesh out its structure. For this reason, Sangiovese-based wines need to be decanted before drinking. It is now also grown as a varietal wine in California.

## TEMPRANILLO

Tempranillo (along with Garnacha) is the main constituent of Spain's quality Rioja wines. It produces rounded examples that are particularly velvety in texture and have a cherry-fruit flavour. These often have a characteristically buttery, vanilla finish, which is a reflection of the prolonged periods they spend maturing in oak casks.

## ZINFANDEL (CALIFORNIA) / PRIMITIVO (ITALY)

A grape variety of Croatian origin, Zinfandel is cultivated predominantly in California and produces a distinctive varietal red wine that is also produced in small quantities in Australia and South Africa. It is the same grape as Primitivo, which is grown in southern Italy. The best examples are sturdy and densely-coloured with a full-body, a medium to high alcohol level and a pronounced blueberry flavour. They benefit from at least half an hour in a decanter before drinking. Zinfandel is also vinified to produce everyday quaffing white and rosé wine styles and like the Syrah grape, often displays a distinct spiciness.

## PINOTAGE

Pinotage is a South African grape which is a crossing between Pinot Noir and Cinsaut (here spelt without an 'l' unlike its French counterpart, Cinsault). It produces wines that are medium in acidity with a deep colour and a jammy fruit flavour.

# Europe's principal grape-growing regions [25]

Old World (or European) wines are generally categorised by their provenance alone and are named after the region or area in which they were made. Crucially, their labels do not usually mention which grape varieties are in their blend. This is because traditionally they were only sold to a domestic market whose customers would already be familiar with their styles. Only knowing their provenance may seem to make it more difficult to choose one Old World wine over another, particularly when comparing them with the consumer-friendly labels of their New World counterparts. But actually, each of Europe's principal grape-growing regions has its own strictly-controlled winemaking regulations and unless a producer chooses to step outside these parameters, the style produced in each region is reasonably consistent and will always contain the same blend of permitted grape varieties that have been vinified in the same way. So through being aware of which grapes are grown where, buying Old World wines becomes as easy as choosing wine according to its grape variety.

# FRANCE

## BORDEAUX

Bordeaux produces predominantly red, long-lived, structured wines that depending on their quality, need from a couple of years at least, to several decades or more to mature before they taste their best. Most of its wines are aged in oak casks, which imbue them with new leather, sandalwood and cinnamon spice aromas. Because of their pronounced structures, they benefit from at least half an hour in a decanter (longer for the very best fine wines) and make great partners to all types of red meat. The dry white wines of Bordeaux are mostly a blend of Sauvignon Blanc and Semillon grape varieties and are easy-drinking wines of no particular distinction. A small amount of Merlot-based rosé wine is also produced, which can be noteworthy in a good vintage.

### MÉDOC (OR LEFT-BANK) R[26]

Within the Médoc is the Haut-Médoc area, the foremost producer of quality wines in the region where four of the five first growths, or 'premier crus'[27] originate: Châteaux Latour, Lafite, Mouton-Rothschild and Margaux. Its wines are predominantly Cabernet Sauvignon-based blends that are generally tannic and structured with blackcurrant fruit flavours and often show hints of stalk or mineral aromas, described as 'rain-on-stones'.

### PESSAC-LÉOGNAN & GRAVES R

This area also produces Cabernet Sauvignon-based blends and is host to the first growth, Château Haut-Brion. Its wines are similar in style to those of the Médoc but are generally fleshier in texture with softer tannins, sweeter fruit and a particular spicy, new leather or cured meat aroma. They are generally of reliable quality and are therefore a good purchasing bet even in challenging vintages. Its white wines are only produced in very small quantities and are extremely sought-after. They are intensely-perfumed, big, oaky and relatively structured with an almost waxy mouthfeel and ripe peach and apricot flavours. Superior quality white and red Graves wines may call themselves 'cru classé' (its wines were classified in 1959).

### ST EMILION & POMEROL (OR RIGHT-BANK) R

These wines are predominantly Merlot and Cabernet Franc-based blends that display a velvety texture and a less pronounced structure than the wines of the left bank. This means they are less long-lived and require less time in a decanter before drinking. (Merlot has a thinner skin than Cabernet Sauvignon and therefore produces wines that are not as tannic). The wines of St Emilion are graded according to their own quality system which is updated roughly every decade. The sixty or so finest properties are ranked either at the top level of 'premier grand cru classé' or at the second 'grand cru classé' level. Those of Pomerol are not ranked at all. In a good vintage, both types of wine show deliciously ripe, sweet, spicy fruit and soft tannins. In a lesser vintage they can be slightly acidic and 'green' or stalky.

### SAUTERNES W[28]

Sauternes is arguably the finest dessert wine-producing region in the world as well as its most famous, thanks to the jewel in its crown, Château d'Yquem[29]. Because the region is criss-crossed by small streams (which produce a humid microclimate that favours the development of noble rot), the wines of Sauternes are distinguished by the complex flavours this produces. The finest wines are produced exclusively from grapes that have been affected by noble rot, whilst lesser wines are made from bunches that may only have been partially-affected. Sauternes wines are luscious, unctuously fat and almost oily in texture with honeyed peachy flavours. Traditionally they are served with foie gras terrine although they can overwhelm this delicate dish. A more unusual but nonetheless delicious partner is a sharp, aged goat's or blue cheese. The very best wines continue to improve over decades.

## BURGUNDY

Burgundy is the home of arguably the finest red (Pinot Noir) and white (Chardonnay) wines of the world, which are supremely elegant, aromatic and capable of lengthy ageing. Lesser wines are produced from the Gamay (red) and Aligoté (white) grapes. The region is large and starts around Auxerre (where the outpost of Chablis is found) then begins again in Dijon, stretching south for 300km until it reaches Lyon. As you travel south and the climate becomes warmer, wines made from the same grape varieties become more fruity, less elegant and fuller-bodied. Vintage variation is significant here as the very best wines are produced in its most northerly sections and as a result, their grapes sometimes struggle to ripen sufficiently.

### CHABLIS W
Chablis is the most northerly Burgundian region and as a result of its microclimate, produces possibly the world's most structured

examples of the Chardonnay grape. These are steely, mineral and high in acidity. Vineyard location is therefore important and the finest 'grand crus' and 'premier crus'[30] vineyards produce the ripest wines. In a good vintage these are golden in colour and deliciously honeyed and yet still retain their mineral aromas and steely acidity. They benefit from decanting at least half an hour before drinking so that their delicate aromas can develop. In a poor vintage Chablis can seem overly acidic, lacking in fruit and bland. Good-value alternatives are the wines from the Petit Chablis areas which produce slightly less austere, riper, more fruity wines that make a good aperitif. Both styles make great partners to seafood and summer salads.

## CÔTE D'OR (CÔTE DE NUITS / CÔTE DE BEAUNE) R & W

This area produces the finest wines of the region. Its white Chardonnay wines (most of which are produced in the more southerly Côte de Beaune area) are exceptionally elegant and are usually fairly lean with a subtle mineral aroma. They possess a graceful acidity and taste both slightly nutty and of apple and pear fruit. Its Pinot Noir reds (the greatest of which are produced in the more northerly Côte de Nuits area) are usually refreshingly acidic and delicately-perfumed and when young display aromatic plum and caramelised red-fruit flavours. As they age these aromas turn slightly vegetal (or as the French describe it, 'animal').

## CÔTE CHALONNAISE / MÂCONNAIS W

Wines from the Mâconnais and Côte Chalonnaise areas are fuller-bodied, less acidic and more buttery in style than their more northerly Côte d'Or counterparts. Their rounded, honeyed Chardonnay white wines (of which the most famous is probably

Pouilly-Fuissé) are better-known than their reds which tend to be more rustic in style. Great-value white wine alternatives can be found in the neighbouring communes of Rully, Montagny, Mercurey and St Véran.

### BEAUJOLAIS R

The Beaujolais region produces predominantly red wines from the Gamay grape. Unfortunately it is notorious for its low quality Beaujolais Nouveau wine, so-called because of its age when commercially released (on the third Thursday of November following the harvest) when it does also produce a number of interesting wines from the 'crus villages' to the north of the region such as Morgon, Côte de Brouilly, Chiroubles and Moulin-à-Vent. These are medium-bodied, quite structured and deliciously fruity and the best are capable of lengthy ageing. They are great served slightly chilled either with cured meats such as carpaccio, with steak tartare, or with barbecued meats.

## LOIRE VALLEY

This elongated wine region starts around Nantes on the west coast of France and extends east for 600km along the length of the river Loire until it reaches the Massif Central. Most famous for its refreshing white wines, it also produces a little Pinot Noir rosé wine and some stalky but elegant Cabernet Franc-based reds. (Both rosé and red wines are really only worth buying in a good vintage because the area is so northerly that their grapes do not ripen sufficiently otherwise). The region's white wines are characterised by their high acidity and should be enjoyed young and fresh. They are particularly delicious served very cold in summer.

## MUSCADET W

Muscadet is produced from the grape of the same name and is generally low in alcohol, extremely lean and very delicately-flavoured with grassy and green apple aromas. In a lesser vintage it can seem bland. In order to gain body and flavour, some wines are left to ferment in contact with their lees[31] for a prolonged period of time. This gives them a slightly yeasty flavour and they are called Muscadet-sur-lie. Others reveal a deliberate residual carbon dioxide, which adds a slight spritziness. Muscadet makes an excellent partner to delicately-flavoured fish or to seafood platters containing oysters, shellfish and crab.

## SANCERRE / POUILLY FUMÉ W

Sancerre and Pouilly-Fumé are probably the best-known Old World examples of the Sauvignon Blanc grape. Whilst most would agree that they are virtually indistinguishable in style, purists claim that the flint soil on which the grapes for Pouilly-Fumé are grown contributes a distinctive edge to its wines. Both are crisp, refreshing examples of the grape and display high acidity with marked herbaceous, elderflower, sweet corn and gooseberry flavours. The slightly fuller-bodied, less structured wines from the neighbouring Quincy and Menetou-Salon areas are great-value quaffing alternatives. All make good partners to fish (particularly smoked) but because of their pronounced gooseberry flavours, can overpower fish that is served with creamy or richly-flavoured sauces. Sancerre also produces a very delicate rosé and red wine from the Pinot Noir grape that is only worth buying in a good vintage.

## BONNEZEAUX / CÔTEAUX DE LAYON W

These superbly luscious, honeyed dessert wines are the Loire Valley's answer to Sauternes. Made from the Chenin Blanc grape, they are high in acidity and therefore capable of lengthy ageing. This also means that they are characteristically refreshing rather than cloying or unctuous.

<hr />

## RHÔNE VALLEY (NORTH AND SOUTH)

The Rhône Valley is made up of two halves: the northern part produces very elegant wines made predominantly from the Syrah grape, whilst those produced in its southern part are blends of a number of grapes and are softer and less elegant but more fruity. Its finest wines improve with age and their high acidity and Syrah-influenced spiciness make them good partners to game, barbecued meats and stews.

### CHÂTEAUNEUF-DU-PAPE R
Châteauneuf-du-Pape is one of the best-known wines from the southern half of the Rhône Valley and is a blend of up to thirteen different grape varieties of which Grenache, Cinsault and Syrah predominate. It is famed for its soil full of pudding stones or 'galets', which store up the heat of the day and radiate it back onto the vine at night thereby mitigating the cool night-time temperatures. Vineyards with a high concentration of pudding stones therefore produce riper grapes than those with none. The finest wines are rich in flavour with a full-body and a high alcohol content whilst there are a number of lesser examples that merely trade off the Châteauneuf-du-Pape brand. (It is important therefore to be aware of the wine's producer when making a purchase). Gigondas and Vacqueyras are relatively recent, up-and-coming wine areas that represent good-value restaurant alternatives. White Châteauneuf-du-Pape is relatively uncommon

and usually made to a high standard. It is big, high in alcohol and has a waxy mouthfeel with a full body and a spicy, white-pepper flavour.

### CÔTES DU RHÔNE R
These wines are generally soft and fruity, easy-drinking Syrah-based blends. They make up the bulk of production for the region and are light enough to be enjoyed without food.

### CÔTE-RÔTIE / HERMITAGE R
Both of these areas produce premium wines. Those from the Côte-Rôtie (or 'roasted slope', which refers to the sun-baked aspect of its vineyards) are supremely elegant Syrah-based examples, partly because up to 20% of their blends can be made up of white wine from the Viognier grape. Hermitage produces the most full-bodied of the Rhône Valley wines and is capable of continuing to improve with age for up to 50 years. Both are great partners to lamb, spicy meats such as sausages, Middle-Eastern food and game.

## SOUTH OF FRANCE[32] (PROVENCE / LANGUEDOC-ROUSSILLON) R & W

The large South of France wine region hugs the Mediterranean coastline and extends from the Pyrenean foothills all the way to Nice. It is made up of two distinct winemaking areas that lie either side of the river Rhône: Provence to the east and Languedoc-Roussillon to the west. The former region is best known for its light but alcoholic, often amber-tinted, fruity rosé wines; the latter produces a number of traditional styles of red wine such as Minervois, Fitou and Corbières. These are made from blends of local grapes and are generally densely-coloured, high in acidity and tannins, and balanced by pronounced spicy fruit flavours that display hints of eucalyptus and tar. They are distinctive wines that provide excellent value for money in a good vintage and which make great partners to grilled or roasted meats, stews and sharp cheeses. In the hands of lesser producers, they can be rustic and lacking in fruit.

## ITALY

### BAROLO / BARBARESCO R

Usually amongst the most expensive Italian options on a wine list, both these wines are impressive and concentrated with high alcohol levels, pronounced aromas of plums and roses, and characteristic hints of 'road tar' and liquorice. Made from 100% Nebbiolo grape variety, they are never very densely-coloured but are highly structured with very high tannins and acidity levels. They therefore require sturdy dishes to stand up to them. Because of their structure, vintage is important and in a bad year they can be lacking in fruit, overly tannic and may even taste bitter. Barbaresco is not quite as full-bodied nor as impressively concentrated as Barolo but both are capable of lengthy ageing. To enjoy them at their best they need at least half an hour in a decanter so that their tannins can soften (even longer for the finest examples).

## BARBERA D'ALBA / D'ASTI R
The Barbera grape produces quality wines in both the Alba and Asti winemaking areas that surround the principal towns of the same name. They are similar in style to France's Beaujolais wine and are easy-drinking in style, light and fruity with refreshingly high acidity. They are best enjoyed young.

## CHIANTI R
Chianti wines are generally medium in colour, high in acidity and characterised by nutty, almost herbal, red fruit flavours. Quality varies greatly within the region so the producer and provenance of the wine is important. Chianti Classico is the best-known wine-producing area and stretches from Florence to Siena. Its wines must be produced exclusively from the Sangiovese grape and are identified by a black cockerel on their label. They are generally more elegant and of a higher quality than the Chianti wines produced in surrounding areas (with the exception of Chianti Rufina). Lesser examples only need a minimum of 75% Sangiovese in their blend and the rest is usually made up of average-quality white wine. Chianti should be enjoyed relatively young unless it is of 'riserva' quality. This means it has been oak and bottle-aged and will continue to improve over a couple of years. Its high acidity makes it a good partner to equally acidic foods such as tomato-based dishes.

## BRUNELLO DI MONTALCINO R
Brunello is a close relative of the Sangiovese grape and produces a rival wine to Barolo in terms of prestige and ageing potential. Montalcino, the town just south of Siena in which it is produced, enjoys a warmer, drier climate than the neighbouring Chianti area so grapes are able to ripen more fully here to produce big,

intense, rich wines that are often very alcoholic and long-lived. These are aged for 48 months prior to release and are therefore best decanted before drinking so that their complex flavours can develop. A softer more accessible version which is only aged for one year prior to release is Rosso di Montalcino.

### VINO NOBILE DI MONTEPULCIANO R

Vino Nobile is another close relative of the Sangiovese grape and its wines are named after the town in which they are produced, Montepulciano. These are similar in style to Chianti riserva but not as elegant; they have a full body and a relatively high alcoholic content.

### VALPOLICELLA / AMARONE DELLA VALPOLICELLA R

Valpolicella is an unsophisticated, easy-drinking wine that is similar in style to Beaujolais. It is light, soft and cherry fruit-flavoured and is best enjoyed young and even chilled. Amarone della Valpolicella is altogether more complex and contains a small percentage of wine made from semi-dried grapes which gives it its characteristic caramelised, dried-fruit aroma. It is an intense, heavy-weight wine that is powerful, deeply-coloured and often high in alcohol, tannins and fruit concentration and as a result, usually sells at premium prices. Most examples are capable of improving with age but lesser-quality versions can sometimes be lacking in acidity and seem rather flabby. Because it is so pronounced in flavour, Amarone is a hard wine to match with food although rich meat stews and tangy cheeses are sufficiently strong to stand up to it. It is also good by itself after a meal as a 'vino di meditazione' (meditation wine). The finest Amarone wines are enhanced by at least three quarters of an hour in a decanter before drinking.

### GAVI W

Gavi is a delicious, refreshingly elegant, highly aromatic wine which has a distinctive steely, citrus finish. It is produced from the indigenous Cortese grape, which has a medium body and a characteristic, honeyed lime flavour. Gavi is a great partner to subtlety-flavoured fish dishes and to mildly-spiced Asian food. It also makes a delicious aperitif.

### ORVIETO / SOAVE W

Orvieto is a common but undistinguished wine that includes the neutral Trebbiano grape in its blend. At best it is soft and easy-drinking with a delicate fruit flavour and hints of almond; lesser-quality examples can be bland. Most Soave is virtually indistinguishable from Orvieto. The less common but superior Soave Classico wine is more fruity, fuller in body and has a slightly steely aroma.

### FRASCATI W

Frascati is a light, fresh, pale-coloured, easy-drinking wine that is best drunk young.

## SPAIN

### RIOJA R

Rioja is probably Spain's best-known wine region and takes its name from the river or 'río', Oja. Its wines are predominantly made from Tempranillo and Garnacha grapes, the latter of which add body to the blend. It can vary greatly in quality depending upon its producer and vintage: in lesser years wines lack fruit concentration and can seem disproportionately acidic. From a good vintage, Rioja is a rich, full-bodied, luscious wine distinguished by its velvety soft mouthfeel and oaky, buttery finish. This is in part due to the length of time it must spend ageing, first in oak cask and then in the bottle, before being released. This period is reflected in the price and name of the wine: the Vino Joven ('young wine') is released the earliest, followed by the Crianza, then the Reserva and then last of all, the Gran Reserva. The finest examples should be decanted for around half an hour before drinking. Rioja makes a great partner to most red and white-meat dishes, stews and cheese, and has sufficiently soft tannins to be enjoyed by itself too.

### PENEDÈS R & W

The Penedès wine region is located in Catalonia, just south-west of Barcelona. It has always been at the centre of the Spanish Cava (sparkling wine) industry but also became the country's most pioneering winemaking region when it improved local practices by growing non-traditional grape varieties, and implemented modern vinification techniques (such as temperature-controlled, stainless steel tanks). As a result, its wines are very clean, elegant and fruity and often include noble varieties such as Chardonnay and Pinot Noir in their blends.

### PRIORAT R

Priorat is also located in Catalonia and produces very high-quality red wines that are rich, spicy, full-bodied and intensely-flavoured. The wines are high in alcohol too and must have a minimum of 13.5%. They are made from a blend of Garnacha and Cariñena (or Carignan), the latter best-known for its role in the spicy, blended wines from the Languedoc area. The quality of Priorat wines depends on their producer and despite usually being very concentrated, they do not necessarily need decanting and are often best enjoyed served straight from the bottle.

### RIBERA DEL DUERO R

This region takes its name from the banks of the river Duero and produces high-quality, full-bodied, elegant red wines, the best of which rival the finest Rioja. Some of these are internationally-renowned and command premium prices such as the wines from producers Vega Sicilia, Pesquera and Alión. The principal grape variety grown here is a local version of Tempranillo, which produces deeply-coloured, highly-structured wines. Non-traditional, Bordeaux varieties are also grown here.

## PORTUGAL

### VINHO VERDE W

The Vinho Verde region is best known for its refreshingly crisp, non-descript, everyday-drinking white wines (because even though far more red wine than white is produced, this is not exported). It displays high acidity and a slight spritziness, which is the result of deliberately-induced residual carbon dioxide. In accordance with its name meaning 'young wine', it is best enjoyed soon after purchase and very chilled. It makes a good summer aperitif.

### DOURO R

Historically more famous for its fortified wine – port – than for its non-fortified wines, this region is named after the river Douro, which is the same river as Spain's Duero. The region now produces some of Portugal's finest and most expensive wines, which are usually made from the same grapes as those used to make port. Over 100 varieties are permitted but Touriga Nacional and Tinta Roriz (which is the same as Spain's Tempranillo) are the most common and produce a wine that shares the tannic, full-bodied, spicy character of a young port. Noble grape varieties such as Cabernet Sauvignon are also being planted in the region.

• – • – •

# GERMANY

### MOSEL-SAAR-RUWER W

Mosel-Saar-Ruwer is Germany's best-known wine region and produces low-alcohol (around 9%), light-bodied, fruity white wines. The best examples are produced from Riesling, the country's premium grape variety. These are often slightly sprizty with high acidity, delicate fruit flavours and a mineral or flint, almost earthy taste. They make good partners to delicately-flavoured fish dishes and are equally delicious by themselves served very cold.

### RHEINGAU W

The Rheingau area also produces wines predominantly from the Riesling grape. These display its characteristically refreshing acidity but are fuller in body and richer in flavour than those from the Mosel. They are thus sufficiently big to provide a great accompaniment to white-meat dishes and to the local, spicy, aromatic, German sausages.

### RHEINHESSEN W

Two different types of wine are produced in the Rheinhessen

region, which is home to many organic and biodynamic winemakers. The first is an easy-drinking style produced predominantly from Muller-Thurgau (Germany's second most planted grape): these are soft and fruity with medium acidity and a slightly floral flavour. The second type is vinified in the Rheinterrasse area and is one of the finest, most elegant examples of Riesling. These are defined by their citrusy, peachy fruitiness and often also show a characteristic hint of smoked meat.

## PFALZ W

This is an up-and-coming region in terms of quality and produces Riesling-based wines that are fullish in body, dry and reasonably alcoholic.

## HOW TO READ A WINE LABEL

*Now that you are able to describe the types of wines you enjoy and are familiar too with both the most common grape varieties for sale as well as the most common wine-producing regions of Europe, you need to be able to use this knowledge to pick one you will like, either from its label or from its description on a wine list. To do this, it is also helpful to know which factors create variations in a wine's taste. These are: its* **country of origin** *(the most important factor), its* **vintage** *and its* **producer.**

*As detailed in the previous section, if a wine is from the New World its grape varieties will be mentioned on its label; if it is from an Old World country, its provenance will usually indirectly reveal its blend. Learning about the characteristics of the world's major grape varieties gives you an idea of a wine's potential flavour. Its country and region of origin then reveal both the type of climate its grapes were grown in (hot or cool), as well as whether it was vinified in a New or Old World way. Both* **climate** *and* **vinification** *have an effect on the final style of wine produced so by taking into account a wine's grape varieties, the climate in which these were grown and the country in which it was vinified, you are in a position to make an informed guess about an unknown wine's style.*

## Climate (Hot vs. Cool)

---

**RULES OF THUMB**

*Hot climates produce straightforward, full-bodied, high-alcohol, tropical fruit-flavoured wines*

*Cool climates produce complex, light to medium-bodied, subtly-flavoured, structured wines*

---

Grapes need a yearly minimum of 1,500 hours' sunshine, 700mm of rain and an average temperature of 10°c in order to ripen satisfactorily. Most commercial vineyards are therefore restricted to the areas that can provide these growing conditions: between 30 and 50° latitude in the northern and southern hemispheres. In the higher latitudes the climate is too cold and damp for vines to ripen; in the lower latitudes it is too hot and there is insufficient rain. Within this band, winemaking regions can be described as enjoying 'hot' or 'cool' climates depending on their proximity to the equator.

Grapes that are grown in relatively hot climates reach sugar maturity very quickly and can therefore be harvested after a shorter 'hang time' (period of time on the vine) than grapes grown under cooler conditions. Hang time allows grapes to develop subtle aromas so wines produced in hotter climates may show a lack of complexity or structure and display predominantly overripe or jammy fruit flavours. Grapes that are grown in relatively cool climates on the other hand, may struggle to ripen and produce enough sugar to balance their acidity. This can result in wines that are low in alcohol and lacking in body and fruit concentration. In both hot and cool climates, the precise location of the vineyards (their altitude, soil type, proximity to water and aspect) and the way in which the vines are managed (whether their foliage is encouraged to provide shade or whether it is cut back to expose the grapes) are key, because they can either mitigate or promote the effects of heat and sunlight.

## Winemaking styles (Old World vs. New World)

> **RULES OF THUMB**
>
> New World wines are usually homogenous in style across producer and vintage: they are uncomplicated and easy-drinking with soft, fleshy textures and pronounced sweet, oaky fruit
>
> Old World wines usually offer a wide range of styles and flavours according to their producer and vintage; they have a pronounced structure (higher tannins and acidity levels) and earthy flavours

European wines are generally vinified according to Old World traditions, which aspire to create the purest expression of the land on which the grapes are grown. Here, each distinct plot of land is thought to have the potential to produce a unique wine even from the same grape variety. Intervention (in the vineyard and cellar) is therefore kept to a minimum in order to promote this notion of 'terroir'. Since most vineyard holdings are small (and generally family-owned), wines produced in the same area may thus differ in style, each expressing their specific terroir and 'aérienne' (rarefied French concept meaning ethereal and skybound).

A wine's provenance reveals the general style in which it was vinified and the techniques its producer subscribes to. This is because regional, European vinous identities are controlled by strict domestic wine laws. These dictate which parts of the land are suitable for vines, the types of grapes that are permitted in each winemaking area, and the way in which the grapes can be vinified. The advantage of this system is that Old World wines tend to have retained their traditional styles and regional diversity over the centuries. Because the industry is still largely made up of small, family-run businesses however (each of which is making wine in the same distinctive way), these methods can be seen as old-fashioned and uncommercial. Indeed, only a select few producers (usually the largest wineries that belong to co-operatives[33] or négociants[34]) are able to afford the latest up-to-date equipment, employ the most prestigious oenologists, and use the most modern techniques to enable them to compete on a national or global level.

The New World winemaking industry was established relatively recently, which means that there is no legacy to preserve and domestic wine laws are relatively lax. Producers therefore enjoy the freedom to experiment with the type of land they cultivate, the grape varieties they grow, and the way in which these are vinified. Since only noble grape varieties boast a global track record, these are the most widely-grown and as a result, commercially-available wine styles tend to be more homogenous and limited in range than in the Old World.

The New World winemaking approach is not focused on the expression of terroir (the concept is less defined here because vineyard holdings tend to be larger and spread over different types of land). It can be defined instead by its focus on winemaking technique and on the maximum extraction of concentrated fruit flavours.

New World producers also differ from Old World producers in that they are more likely to have chosen the industry rather than to have been born into it. As a result, they are often wealthier at the outset and therefore benefit from better access to technological know-how and modern equipment. New World producers are thus well placed to respond to consumer wine trends and tend to produce wines that are more commercial in style and easier to appreciate with pronounced, ripe fruit and oaky flavours.

## Vintage & Producer

---

### RULES OF THUMB

Vintage variation is area-specific and is most evident in cool-climate, red wines

A producer has more influence on wine style in a cool-climate, Old World country than in a hot-climate, New World country

The price of a wine reflects the quality of its vintage and the skill of its producer

---

Each area within a winemaking region enjoys a specific microclimate. This means that vintage variation is neither uniform across a country nor a region. Thus a good vintage for red Bordeaux will not necessarily be a good vintage either for Chianti or for red Burgundy. Likewise within the Bordeaux region, wines from the St Emilion area may be of a higher quality overall than those from the Médoc because of their different microclimates and because of the differing ripening requirements of the grapes grown in each area.

Rather than memorise vintage charts relevant to particular regions, you can usually rely on the price of a wine compared to that of other vintages of same type to indicate its relative quality. Vintage variation is more noticeable in wines from cool climates, where annual weather patterns are less predictable than in hot-climate countries. It is especially apparent in wines that come from areas with a marginal climate, where a bad vintage means grapes may not ripen at all. Vintage is also more relevant when choosing red rather than white wines because the resulting marked structure and lack of fruit produced by a bad one are arguably more palatable in a white wine (which will display high acidity, delicate fruit flavours and which will most probably just taste rather bland) than in a red wine (which will also display high acidity but unripe or 'green' fruit flavours and chewy tannins too). Red wines from a poor vintage in the Loire Valley for example, will therefore suffer more in relative quality than its white wines.

The difference in quality between producers is usually more marked in Old World rather than New World wines because of the sheer concentration of producers in one particular European winemaking area. This is especially evident in Burgundy, where smallholdings have progressively shrunk over the generations[35] and where just one vineyard may now have over twenty owners. Since Old World producers are bound by the same regional winemaking regulations, it is easier to make a direct quality comparison here than it is to do so amongst producers from the same region in a New World country.

When buying high-end, fine wines it is useful to research who the best producers of each type are before making an expensive mistake. If you are faced with a range of producers or vintages of the same type of wine and are unsure which to choose, a consistently reliable option is a wine that is co-operative or négociant-produced. It is unlikely to be exceptional in quality and will probably be generic in style, but will usually be fairly-priced.

# TOP WINE TIPS

## ENJOYING WINE

*Now that you are able to make an informed guess about the potential style of an unfamiliar wine by taking into consideration its grape varieties, climate and winemaking techniques, the first half of Section Two concentrates on enhancing your appreciation of it: it demonstrates how a wine's flavour can be influenced by external factors (how you can improve an average bottle and make the most out of a great one), how to pair wine with food, how to spot if a wine is off, as well as how best to store it.*

# Serving it

The way in which a wine is served will influence its taste: the
type of glassware used (as well as how this has been cleaned), the
temperature of the wine, whether it has been decanted or not, the
type of food it is paired with and the order in which it is served –
all have a unique effect on your overall impression of it.

## GLASSWARE

A wine's bouquet can easily be overpowered by other smells so
glassware should be perfectly clean, particularly when drinking
delicately-perfumed, fine wines. To prevent them gathering dust,
the best way to store wine glasses is upside down. This can
however imbue them with a musty smell so it is best to rinse
them before use with warm water using a minimum amount of
detergent and either leave them to drip dry (this is preferable) or
dry them with a clean dishcloth. (Both detergent and dishcloths
can leave a glass with unwanted aromas and in the case of
sparkling wines, detergent will ruin the quality of the bubbles).

The type of glassware you use is mainly an aesthetic choice
although certain designs can enhance or detract from the style of
wine they contain, primarily by influencing the surface area that
is exposed to air. Red wines for example are enhanced more by a
wide bowl than by a narrow flute-shape because the former gives
them the additional exposure they need for their tannins to
soften. Likewise wines that are heavily-perfumed are best enjoyed
in a glass with a squat, balloon-shaped bowl as this encourages
their complex flavour compounds to develop and gather at the
rim of the glass.

The ideal wine-glass shape is that of a tulip because it funnels the wine's aromas towards your nose. The width of the bowl in comparison to the rim, the height of the bowl and even the thickness of the glass then vary the degree to which this occurs – it is said that the thinner the glass, the more sensual the experience can be. According to purists such as the specialist glass-maker Riedel, it is the minute adjustments to these design attributes which adapt a glass to work in harmony with the particular aromas of a specific grape variety. This is achieved by channelling the grape's unique set of characteristics towards the specific sensory areas in the nose or mouth that appreciate them most. (They therefore stock several ranges of glasses, each of which offers one glass suited to a particular grape variety or common blend).

The stem of a glass also has an effect on your perception of a wine and a tall, thin stem is not only more elegant but also serves the purpose of creating a distance between your hand and the wine so that the latter isn't unduly affected by body heat. That said, stem-less wine tumblers are currently very fashionable!

Whatever its size or shape, a glass should only ever be filled to one third. This provides room for the wine's aromas to concentrate and allows you to swirl it in the glass to expose it further to air, without spilling it.

### TEMPERATURE

Most wines are served between 6 to 18°C although in summer or in a hot climate where the ambient temperature is relatively high and they warm up quickly, it is best to serve them very cold. The perfect serving temperature varies depending on whether you wish either to enhance a wine's qualities or to mask its faults. It also depends upon cultural preference – the French prefer to serve red wine at a cooler temperature than the English as well as drink it after a shorter ageing period.

Temperatures near the higher end of the serving range will enhance a wine's flavour by encouraging its volatile flavour compounds to evaporate. Cooler temperatures have the opposite effect and can make an otherwise aromatic wine seem closed; complex wines should therefore be served relatively warm. Tannic wines should also be served relatively warm but for different reasons – because the cold exaggerates this characteristic and can make a wine seem more bitter than it actually is. Conversely, both red and white, inexpensive or flabby wines should be served relatively cold so that they seem more structured and refreshing.

Serving temperature also affects the perceived sweetness of a wine: the higher the temperature, the sweeter it will seem. So if a sweet wine is lacking in acidity (acidity is desirable in order to offset its unctuousness), its apparent sweetness can be diminished by serving it very cold. Spicy and grilled foods are best complemented by slightly chilled wines whereas foods that are more delicately-flavoured are best paired with wines served slightly warm.

### AERATING & DECANTING
Merely removing the cork from a bottle to let the wine 'breathe' before drinking it does not achieve a great deal. This is because the amount of wine that is exposed to air through doing so amounts to only a tiny proportion of what is in the bottle. To aerate a wine properly you need to decant it. This means pouring

it from the bottle into another vessel which is then used to pour it into glasses. A decanter can be purely decorative or it can serve to measure out a specific amount of wine (as in the 25, 50 and 100cl 'pichets' or jugs found in European restaurants).

Whether a wine actually needs to be aerated or not is a matter of preference and experience. Aeration serves to speed up the ageing process and soften a wine if it is either too acidic or too tannic by encouraging its fruit flavours to emerge. Most everyday-drinking wines will benefit from some exposure to air but too long in a decanter and their fruit characteristics will fade. As a general rule: everyday-drinking wines are enhanced by being decanted just prior to drinking whereas mature red wines or fine white wines benefit from a slightly longer exposure to air. (When aerating a fine white wine it is best to decant it first then place the decanter itself into the fridge in order to keep the wine cool. Be careful to cover the top of the decanter so that the wine doesn't absorb other fridge smells).

If you are unsure as to how long to decant a wine for, it is best to do so for less time than it needs than to ruin it through over-exposure. This is because it will be aerated further every time it is poured into a glass and will continue to be exposed to air during the time it takes you to drink it. Half an hour is therefore a good starting point for most wines. Alternatively you could use 'oxygenizing' glasses or filters: the former claim to let a wine breathe whilst it is in the glass via the glass itself, apparently achieving in 2-4 minutes what a decanter achieves in 1-2 hours; the latter aerate a wine as it is poured through the filter into a glass.

Decanting a red wine properly can also potentially enhance its flavour by filtering out any sediment that may have drifted to the bottom of the bottle. Unless the wine is faulty, most sediment is made up of colour pigment, tannins and tartrates (harmless crystalline deposits made up of dead yeast and leftover grape pulp) which have not been filtered out during the fining process. These allow it to continue to gain in complexity as it ages. Sediment is therefore only found in mature red wines. To remove it, it must first have settled at the bottom of the bottle so that you can see it trickling past the neck when you are pouring the wine into a decanter. The best way to do this is by placing a lit candle just underneath the neck so that when the darker, grainy-looking particles are highlighted, you know when to stop. This should occur when you have decanted nearly all of the wine and normally leaves you with around half an inch in the bottle. A delicate wine should be poured down the side of the decanter rather than directly into it so that the bottle is not emptied too violently (this will adversely affect its flavour). The remaining wine can be decanted again once the sediment has re-settled at the bottom.

**SERVING ORDER**
The order in which a selection of wines is served affects their comparative taste: a delicately-perfumed wine will seem bland if preceded by a big, tannic one for example. The traditional serving order is governed by a wine's strength of flavour and usually follows its colour, acidity and sweetness, as well as whether it is sparkling or not. Thus sparkling wine, which is usually the least pronounced in fruit flavour and the highest in acidity is usually served first, followed by white wine, rosé, red and finally sweet dessert wine.

When serving more than one wine of the same colour, light, aromatic wines should always be served before full-bodied, structured ones that display either a lot of oak or pronounced aromas. Likewise, wines that are high in acidity should be served before those that are not, and wines that are low in tannins and lightly-coloured should be served before those that are high in tannins and deeply-coloured. Furthermore, older vintages and Old World wines (both of which are more likely to be delicately-flavoured, aromatic and complex) should be served before younger vintages of the same wine or New World examples (which are likely to show more dominant fruit flavours). You should be able to guess the style of a wine from what you know of its grape varieties and provenance but if you are unsure, it is best to taste the entire selection prior to deciding on a serving order.

# Food pairing

Food can either enhance or have a detrimental effect on the taste of a wine. It is therefore important to know how to pair it. The easiest way to start is by categorising both the dish and the wine according to its 'type' of flavour. For example is the dish in question: light or heavy, creamy or sour, full-flavoured or bland, spicy or mild? Likewise is the wine light, acidic and refreshing, full-bodied, tannic and alcoholic, or is it medium-bodied and delicately-perfumed? As a general rule: the dish will be a good match for the wine if it either mirrors or shares its type. Thus a fragrant, spicy Indian curry would complement an equally aromatic, spicy, pronounced wine (made from either Gewürztraminer or Riesling for example) and a smoked salmon dish would make a good partner to either an oaky wine such as a white Rioja or to an oaked Sauvignon Blanc. Alternatively a rich, sweet, full-bodied Sauternes dessert wine would be perfectly complemented by its mirror image in the form of an acidic Roquefort blue cheese. This last example also demonstrates that whilst tradition dictates both that red wine is the best match for meat and cheese and that white wine should be drunk with fish, this is not always the case. Indeed certain fish dishes are best complemented by aromatic red wines such as those made from Pinot Noir, many cheeses are enhanced by full-bodied white wines, and both white-meat dishes and Asian foods are so versatile they can be paired with either white or red wines.

Another useful food-pairing rule is that a wine should be weighty enough in terms of fruit flavour and structure to stand up to the dish with which it is being paired. Furthermore its acidity levels should provide a balance to the food's fat content and the wine should mirror its richness. So a creamy dish should be served with an equally richly-flavoured, full-bodied wine but one that also has reasonably high acidity levels (such as a full-bodied Chardonnay or Viognier). Likewise dishes that are high in fat content such as either roast duck, lamb or foie gras are enhanced by fruity, aromatic, high acidity wines that cut through the fat and provide a refreshing counterbalance.

Unfortunately, certain foods are notoriously difficult to pair with wine despite these general guidelines, either because they are difficult to categorise by type or because they have an effect on the palate which makes wine taste odd: for example artichokes, asparagus and sashimi can make wine seem metallic; vinegar-based dressings and peanuts tend to destroy a wine's flavours altogether; olives can overpower a wine's aromas; spinach can make red wine taste rusty, and neither eggs nor avocado seem to go with any style of wine. It is therefore best to pair these kinds of foods with the beverage with which they have traditionally been enjoyed such as sake or green tea alongside sashimi and sherry alongside olives.

# Wine faults

Not all wine 'faults' indicate that a wine is off. A few can render a wine completely undrinkable, in which case you are justified in asking for a replacement. But some are harmless and have no effect on its taste and others may only slightly alter a wine's flavour and not necessarily in an unpleasant way.

The majority of wine faults can be detected without tasting it. Tasting merely confirms or allays any concerns you might have as well as revealing whether the wine is off-dry – this is the only thing that can be detected through taste alone. Some wine faults are obvious from its appearance but most are detected by smelling it. So when you are offered a sample in a restaurant or bar before a full glass is poured, you need only to sniff the wine to check whether it is off. (Contrary to what you might think, you are not in fact being asked whether you like it because even if you don't, you can't ask for an alternative purely on these grounds).

Below is a list of common wine faults which includes the way in which they can be spotted, possible causes, the degree to which they are likely to have affected the wine's flavour and structure, as well as how if at all they can be remedied.

**BUBBLES**
If there are bubbles in a still wine, this is because it has continued to ferment and to produce carbon dioxide after it has been bottled. This gas remains dissolved in solution until the bottle is opened. In a mature, particularly red wine, bubbles are considered

a fault and show that the wine is unstable. They are usually the result of insufficient filtration or stabilisation[36] prior to bottling. In a young white wine on the other hand, a slight effervescence is more likely to have been deliberately induced in order to give it a refreshing zest than to be considered to be a fault. (This is the case with some Portuguese white wines such as Vinho Verde and some French Muscadet-sur-lie). If you are unsure as to whether the presence of bubbles means the wine is unstable or not, it is best to taste it to see if they enhance or spoil your enjoyment of it.

## CLOUDINESS

All wines are stabilised to a certain degree and should always therefore be clear and bright. Fine wines however are filtered less than everyday-drinking wines (so as not to strip them of their more delicate aromas) and residual suspended particles may sometimes make these seem relatively cloudy. If you are presented with a cloudy wine, you should leave it to stand in the glass for a while to see if the haze settles. If it remains cloudy after a period of time, the wine may be off. This may be due either to the growth of yeast or bacteria, or because the wine was vinified in copper or brass pipes. If the haze has an adverse affect on the wine's bouquet or flavour, you should ask for a replacement.

## SEDIMENT

There are different types of wine sediment. The most common is made up of deposits, including dead yeast cells, grape pulp, tannins and colour pigments. This type is usually found in quality red wines that have matured over a long period of time. It is harmless but may have a bitter taste and can therefore be filtered off by decanting the wine.

Another type of sediment is that formed by tartaric crystals, which you will find at the bottom of either the wine bottle or your glass once it has been poured, or attached to the underside of the cork. Because they are naturally colourless, they can resemble shards of glass in a white wine but in a red wine they absorb its colour and are less noticeable. Tartaric crystals are more commonly found in wines produced in cool regions because of their relatively high levels of tartaric acid. Since this is more soluble in grape juice than it is in wine, it is often precipitated out of solution after fermentation to form these harmless crystals.

Finding bits of cork in a wine does not mean that the wine is corked. It may however mean that the bottle has been stored upright for a prolonged period of time (rather than on its side whereby the cork remains in constant contact with the wine and therefore remains moist). This is likely to cause a cork to dry out and crumble when drawing it out of the bottle. If the wine also has an orangey colour and smells of port or madeira, the wine is probably either oxidised or maderised (see below).

## CORK TAINT

Cork taint is caused by compounds released by fungi naturally present in cork. The reasons behind this are still unknown. As the term suggests, it only occurs in wines sealed with a cork and approximately 5% of these will suffer from cork taint. In order to avoid this risk altogether, more and more wineries are turning to alternative stoppers such as plastic corks and screw caps.

A wine that has been affected by cork taint smells musty and slightly mouldy, like wet cardboard or an old book. (A similar but less pungent odour is caused by the heavy-handed use of sulphur-dioxide during the stabilisation of a wine. This is usually more noticeable in white rather than red wine). There are different degrees of cork taint and sometimes it is hard to pick up just by smelling a wine. It is often more noticeable on the palate because it usually cancels out most of the wine's fruit aromas and also cuts short its length. Sometimes the corked aroma will dissipate when you swirl the wine but it can also grow more pronounced as the wine is exposed to air. Adding a small amount of uncorked wine or port and mixing the two can help mask the corky aroma; alternatively, weird as it may seem, macerating a ball of cling film in the wine usually diminishes it!

A slight cork taint does not always render a wine undrinkable, indeed people seem to vary in their sensitivity to it (it is said that women both pick up on it more readily and find it less acceptable than men). Nonetheless if the aroma is detectable, you are justified in asking for a replacement in a bar or restaurant. Unfortunately this is not possible if you purchased the wine from a retail outlet because corkiness is not a man-made fault and therefore cannot be attributed to either the producer or seller of the wine.

### OXIDATION

Oxidation is the result of over-exposure to air and severe oxidation turns a wine to vinegar. This is an age-old problem that has presented a challenge to the effective storage and vinification of wine throughout history. (In Roman times, tree resin was added to wine amphorae in an attempt to prevent it, and a modern example of this legacy is Greece's resinated Retsina wine). Barrel and bottle stoppers are today's answer to prevention because they provide an air-tight seal but this only works when the bottle stoppers are kept moist and the barrels fully topped up. This is why it is best to store a wine bottle on its side. If it is kept upright, the cork will not only slowly lose moisture and dry out but it will also eventually shrink and then gradually let unwanted oxygen in.

Oxidation is detectable in a wine's appearance, smell and taste: it turns both white and red wines orange or brown and produces port-like or stewed aromas on the nose and palate. A wine that is oxidised therefore no longer tastes fresh but unlike one that is corked, the result is not necessarily entirely unpleasant. Indeed a slight degree of oxidation may even improve a thin wine and turn it into a good partner to cheese. Alternatively you could try it as a dessert wine. If however it has adversely affected the wine's taste, you would be justified in asking for a replacement in a restaurant as well as from a retail outlet (provided the oxidation was not caused by inadequate bottle storage on your part).

## MADERISATION

If a wine is maderised, it is usually brownish in colour and smells and tastes like madeira (the fortified wine produced on the island of the same name). The effect is not always unpleasant and a slight degree of maderisation can sometimes even improve a wine by adding caramelised aromas. (If this is the case, it can be enjoyed as a dessert wine or paired with cheese). The fault is caused by exposure both to excess oxygen and to prolonged high temperatures. Wine is very sensitive to fluctuations in temperature and ideal wine storage conditions are a relatively cool 14°C. As with an oxidised wine, if a maderised wine tastes unpleasant, you are entitled to ask for a replacement in a restaurant as well as from a retail outlet, provided the fault was not caused by you.

**COOKED WINES**

A cooked wine is usually the result of either poor storage or of transportation at high or fluctuating temperatures. Like a maderised wine, it is usually brownish in colour and smells and tastes caramelised, burnt or similar to port. There are often additional, external signs that a wine has been cooked: the bottle may have a stained label, a sticky foil cap or low ullage – all of which would indicate that the wine was heated sufficiently to rise up through the cork and trickle down the sides of the bottle. The fact that a wine is cooked is justification for asking for a replacement in a restaurant or from a retail outlet, provided the fault was not caused by you. At home, you can use it as a cooking ingredient.

## Storing it

Most wines are vinified for drinking within a couple of years of bottling (although their ageing potential can be enhanced in the cellar by fermenting or vinifying them in wooden barrels instead of in stainless steel tanks.) The tannic content of red wine ensures that it will usually last longer than white wine but only a small percentage requires ageing before it reaches its peak. Generally these are fine wines which possess the required high levels of both acidity and sugar (and in the case of red wines, high tannin levels too).

### AGEING

The exact chemical process that occurs during ageing remains relatively unclear but what is known is that short-term storage results in a wine that is more complex in flavour, softer and less astringent. When kept for too long, a wine will start to lose its fruit flavours, its acidity levels will begin to dominate its structure (even though they actually remain the same throughout its life) and eventually it will turn into vinegar.

It is not possible to tell whether a wine has reached its peak-drinking period or not without opening it, unless the bottle glass is clear or lightly-coloured and the wine is so past its optimum drinking phase that its orangey colour is evident. (As detailed in the first section, you can judge a wine's maturity by its appearance: red wines get paler as they age whereas white wines get darker). Identifying the moment at which a wine with ageing potential will taste its best is therefore difficult, not only because it goes through various stages as it matures (including a period

where it may taste closed and very disappointing) but also
because different bottles of the same wine may mature at
different rates, even when stored under identical conditions. This
is called bottle variation and is usually the result of more than
one bottling batch (the wines in each may have been treated
slightly differently during their vinification and maturation
periods). It may also be a reflection of the quality of individual
corks. It is therefore usually best to err on the side of caution and
store a wine for less time than is perhaps advised rather than let
it spoil. If it tastes a little young when you open it, you can
artificially speed up the ageing process by decanting it.

Whether a wine spoils or not during its maturation depends a
great deal on how it is stored – fluctuations in temperature,
humidity, light and movement can all have an adverse effect on
its final quality. Unless you own a wine cellar or a specialist wine
fridge, professional warehouse storage is advisable for fine wines
which need prolonged cellaring. There, wines can be stored either
under bond[37] or duty paid[38] and you are charged a fee per case
per year. Before paying for this service however, it is important to
check not only that the warehouse is adequately covered against
a potential flood or fire, but also that each individual case is
marked with a coded reference number that refers to you as the
owner. This means that the storage company or wine merchant
from whom you purchased the wine is merely the custodian and
if either should go out of business, the wine cannot be held
against the value of the company and remains yours.

TEMPERATURE & LIGHT
Storage temperature probably has the greatest influence on
eventual wine quality because it affects the speed of the chemical

reactions that cause a wine to age: the cooler the conditions, the slower the rate at which the wine matures and the more complex the resulting wine; warm temperatures on the other hand, encourage the development of jammy or cooked flavours which can overpower its structure.

An ideal storage temperature is around 14°C, which is roughly that of a cellar or specialist wine fridge. A normal fridge on the other hand, is an adequate storage facility either for the very short term (weeks not months) or for both red and white wines that have already been opened (the cold slows down the rate at which the wines turn to vinegar). It is not suitable for long-term storage because it may vibrate slightly and its atmosphere is too dry for corks. Everyday-drinking wine can be stored at room temperature for a limited period of time but fluctuations caused by central heating, air-conditioning or infrequent sunshine will quickly cause the wine to spoil.

Ultra-violet light is harmful too so wines should neither be stored in direct sunlight nor under strong artificial lighting (both of which also generate unwanted heat). Ideally they should be placed in a dark location such as a cool cupboard or cellar. This is why wine fridges have either no glass or tinted glass doors and why most wine bottles are made of dark glass.

## MOVEMENT & HUMIDITY

Movement can accelerate the ageing process by shaking up the oxygen that is naturally dissolved in wine. It can also cause a fine red wine to taste bitter by shaking up the tannins and other suspended particles in it (although you can reverse this first by letting the bottle stand and then by carefully decanting the wine).

Excessive movement leads to a phenomenon called bottle sickness, which results in a wine tasting off or 'unclean'. You should therefore always allow a wine to rest upright before drinking it, particularly if it has recently been transported from one location or country to another.

Humidity most affects the quality of wines stoppered with a cork and even if this is kept moist by storing the bottle on its side, an environment that is too dry will gradually cause the cork to shrink. Unwanted oxygen then seeps in, speeding up the ageing process and eventually causing the wine to become oxidised. An environment that is too humid on the other hand, may cause wine labels to go mouldy. This does not affect the wine's quality but it can influence its re-sale or investment value, particularly in markets that value the pristine such as China.

# BUYING WINE

*The second half of Section Two helps you decide where to buy your wine and illustrates the differences between the various retail options open to you. It also explains whether a wine's bottle shape, colour and stopper affect its style, whether wine medals and awards actually mean anything, and whether wine is a viable alternative investment, giving you an insight into how the elusive wine auction and 'futures' markets work.*

# Where to go

As wine has grown in popularity worldwide, so too has the amount and range of styles produced. The number of outlets that sell wine has also grown so it is useful to know the differences between the ranges offered by each as well as the advantages and disadvantages of buying wine from them: supermarkets, wine merchants, off-licences, auction houses and online vendors are distinguished not only by their selections but also by their mark-ups, the potential condition of their wines and by the professional advice and value-added services they may or may not provide.

## SUPERMARKETS

Supermarket chains are distinguished from other wine retail outlets by their buying power. They have the highest wine turnover of all (selling nearly three quarters of all bottles drunk in the UK) and are therefore able to obtain the lowest purchase prices from producers as well as have the biggest say in the types of wines that they would like created. This means that of all the places in which you can buy wine, supermarkets usually offer the largest range of good-value, everyday-drinking examples, especially in the form of generic own-brand labels. They also offer a good selection of less commercial wines from up-and-coming regions that smaller wine outlets may not be in a position to risk stocking. Doing so is less chancy for a supermarket because wine is not their only source of revenue, plus most chains have sophisticated logistical networks which allow them to import wines from countries that may be too obscure or remote for a smaller, stand-alone outlet to be able to justify financially.

The size of a supermarket can also be a disadvantage however, because the chain will require a large amount of a certain wine in order to stock its network of stores. This means that they are unable to represent some smaller boutique producers who cannot fulfil this demand. Another disadvantage of buying wine from a supermarket is that there are usually no specialist staff on hand to offer advice nor any value-added services available. So for everyday purchases, the supermarket wins in terms of pricing and convenience but if you are not sure what you want to buy and want to spend a little over the minimum, a specialist shop is usually a better alternative.

## SPECIALIST WINE SHOPS & OFF-LICENCES

Specialist wine shops can either be independent or form part of a chain. If the chain is large, it will suffer from the same disadvantages as a supermarket – it may be limited to offering purely commercial wines that are produced on a scale that is large enough to supply all of its outlets. Since specialist shops are usually located in town centres their overheads are high and this may be reflected in their slightly inflated prices. This also means however that they need a hook to lure customers in off the street, and this may take the form of special offers such as a discount for buying a case of twelve bottles or more, specially-priced bin-ends or regular in-store tastings (which are a great way to broaden your wine knowledge for free).

Buying wine from a specialist shop is a good option if you are not sure what type of wine you are looking for because shop staff might not necessarily be experts, but should be sufficiently knowledgeable to be able to recommend wines that fit your budget and tastes. Their selection is often wider than in a supermarket both in terms of price and the type of producer they represent, and usually includes a selection of fine wines too. As a result, their clientele tends to be reasonably discerning and experimentation is encouraged by their wine presentation, which often includes a numerical score or a brief description of wine style.

## WINE MERCHANTS

Most wine merchants work exclusively from offices although some also have retail outlets and even wine bars. They are usually not as commercial in their range as either supermarkets or large specialist chains and are often small enterprises whose strengths lie in their expert knowledge and value-added services. These might include tailored customer cellar plans, advice on wine investments and brokerage, delivery of wines to your home, access to professional storage facilities and to buying wine 'en primeur'[39], as well as invitations to exclusive events, new vintage launches and tastings. Merchants may also act as the agents for a number of 'trophy'[40] wines, which means they are the only ones to import them into the country. (They sell these wholesale to other merchants as well as directly to private clients). They therefore take great care to cultivate their relationships with châteaux and wine suppliers in order to gain favourable allocations for their clients.

Wine merchants probably offer the widest selection of wines of any outlet and stock a range of quality and price from good-value everyday-drinking wines all the way to top-end wines. Because they are not demanding in terms of quantity of stock required, their particular forte is the representation of small, boutique producers and fine wines.

## WINE CLUBS

Membership of a wine club is usually available in conjunction with membership of something that is non wine-related such as a bank or a magazine. This carries a fee and is usually for a minimum period of time, during which wines are delivered either to you or to professional storage on a regular basis and at a discounted rate. The advantage of joining lies in the hassle-free method of building a collection and the fact that you are forced to expand your tasting range and experience through the selection of wine that is provided for you.

The disadvantage of relying on a wine club for your purchases is that you may receive more wine than you can drink (if for example you either travel frequently or also buy your own wine stocks) and they may not be suitable for laying down to enjoy at a later stage (particularly if the supplier is using the club as a means to keep his stocks in check). This means you run the risk of being lumbered with wines that will spoil before you have had a chance to enjoy them. Furthermore without knowing what kind of selection criteria they are following, the wines they provide may not be to your liking. It is therefore best to research a wine club thoroughly before joining to make sure that membership will suit you. You can do this by asking for a list of previous years' deliveries and then checking whether these types of wines would appeal to you. An alternative to membership is to set aside the amount of money you would have paid each month to a wine club and use this to purchase your own mixed cases instead, along your own time lines.

## WINE PRODUCERS

Purchasing wines directly from their producer is an option that is gaining in popularity, particularly for travellers visiting wine-making regions. There are several advantages in doing so: the wines are usually cheaper than when bought direct from a retail outlet, they may not be available where you live, and in addition to a purchase of wine, visitors may also enjoy a tour of the winery and a chat with the producer.

New World winemakers in particular have embraced the commercial potential that wine tourism presents and realising that just as much money can be made from additional wine-related activities as from straightforward sales, many have developed their wineries to include restaurants, hotels and in some cases even wine spas. As a result, certain wine regions – such as California's Napa Valley, Australia's Margaret River or South Africa's Constantia – have blossomed into destinations in their own right.

The disadvantage of buying from a producer is that you may have to transport the wines home yourself, and you may be limited by the local wine authorities to purchasing only a certain amount. There may be additional duties or taxes too which need to be paid when the wine is taken out of the state or country in which it was bought. It is therefore important to research all this before travelling to a winery expressly to make a purchase, in order to assess whether it truly is advantageous or not.

AUCTION HOUSES

The majority of wines bought and sold by auction houses have a secondary market, meaning they are either fine, rare, or have investment potential. Fine wines are often brands in their own right and therefore appeal to a global market. They also make attractive potential investment purchases because they are only produced in limited quantities. This means that their value often increases as stocks diminish. Because fine wines are capable of ageing over a considerable length of time, they also increase in value as they reach their peak maturity. Beyond this point, the finest may even continue to increase in value as they become rarer still.

The main advantage of buying from an auction house is the access it provides to these unusual or rare wines that may not otherwise still be available on the market. Often these have been sourced directly from private collectors or estates. The majority of buyers at auction are members of the wine trade who buy in order to sell the stock on. Because of this, auction prices are the lowest on the market and there are considerable bargains available. If a wine is particularly popular however, it may provoke a bidding war and the final 'hammer price' may actually result in being higher than its actual market price, indeed even more so once the hidden costs of buyers' premium, delivery and taxes have been added. (It is therefore important to bear this in mind when you consider placing a bid).

The disadvantage of buying at auction is the lack of purchasing advice available and buyers need to be familiar with the differences in quality between various vintages and producers that are reflected in the bidding estimates. Estimates are also affected by the condition of the wines being sold: if it is either less than acceptable for its age or if the bottle's outwardly appearance is felt to have a potentially detrimental effect on the buyer's ability to sell it on, this information will be included in the auction catalogue notes. These may detail the wine's ullage[41], the quality of the bottle capsule, whether the cork is raised or not, the state of its label (whether this is stained or torn), whether the bottle shows signs of having leaked, and most importantly whether it has been imported or has travelled overseas at some point (proof of this is an import or strip-label glued to the bottle).

## ONLINE VENDORS

Purchasing wine online offers the same advantage as purchasing any other product on the internet – it is convenient and may also be cheaper because an online shop has lower overheads than a retail outlet. The principal disadvantage of doing so is also true of any other product bought online: because it isn't tangible, opportunities for fraud are more easily exploited than in a shop. This is particularly true of fine or rare wines that have a premium value. Since the wine trade is not regulated, it is important to check the reputation of the online merchant carefully before making a purchase, especially if they do not also have a retail presence or registered office. It is also worth comparing prices with other retail outlets to verify that those from an online vendor are in line with the market (www.winesearcher.com is a useful website).

# What to look for

A wine bottle's size, shape, weight, colour and stopper may vary. These differences may or may not have a bearing on the quality of the wine inside so it is important to be able to distinguish between those that do affect its style and taste, and merely aesthetic variations in presentation.

## BOTTLE SIZE

Bottle sizes vary enormously and range from the smallest (usually plastic) 100ml bottles on offer on airlines or trains, to the largest, rarely-produced melchior and sovereign formats that hold the equivalent of 24 or 34 standard bottles of wine respectively. Before the EU regulated sizes in the 1970s, the most popular held between 650 to 850ml of wine. (This was supposed to reflect the average lung capacity of a glass blower). Today the standard bottle size is 750ml although in non-EU countries such as Switzerland, the arguably more practical 500ml size bottle is commoner.

Bottle size is significant particularly in wines meant for ageing because it affects the speed at which the wine inside matures. This is partly because the amount of air left between the wine and the cork is always the same regardless of size (because the neck of the bottle retains the same dimensions) so that in a larger format bottle this amounts to a smaller percentage of the total wine being exposed. Since it is exposure to air that accelerates a wine's ageing process, it follows that wines mature more slowly and with greater finesse in large bottle formats. This is why they are preferred over standard sizes for wines with ageing potential such as fine claret.

In France, larger format bottles have specific names. Confusingly, the same name may refer to different sizes depending on the provenance of the wine it contains. Bordeaux, Burgundy and Champagne regions offer the largest formats:

| Name of bottle format (according to region) | | Bottle size |
|---|---|---|
| BORDEAUX | BURGUNDY/CHAMPAGNE | |
| Half Bottle | Half Bottle | Half bottle (375ml) |
| Bottle | Bottle | Bottle (750ml) |
| Magnum | Magnum | 2 bottles (1.5l) |
| Marie-Jeanne | — | 3 bottles (2.25l) |
| Double magnum | Jéroboam | 4 bottles (3l) |
| Jéroboam | Rehoboam | 6 bottles (4.5l) |
| Impériale | Methusela | 8 bottles (6l) |
| — | Salmanazar | 12 bottles (9l) |
| — | Balthazar | 16 bottles |
| — | Nebuchadnezzar | 20 bottles |
| — | Melchior | 24 bottles |
| — | Sovereign | 34 bottles |

## BOTTLE SHAPE, WEIGHT & COLOUR

The shape of a bottle can vary in height, in width and in the slope of its 'shoulder' (the area between the neck and the widest part of the bottle. This is where ullage is measured in Bordeaux-shaped bottles). Its shape is not indicative of the quality of wine inside but may give you a clue as to its style. This is because historically certain bottle shapes have become associated with wines from certain regions. France's Bordeaux and Burgundy regions for example, have traditionally used differently-shaped bottles: wines from the former (bar a few exceptions) use bottles with a shortish neck and squareish shoulders whereas wines from the latter are produced in bottles with a longer neck and sloping shoulders. German producers have also traditionally stuck to a distinctive bottle shape that is very tall with an unusually long, thin neck. Producers from other regions sometimes adopt these shapes in order to be associated with the prestige of those particular wines. Some Spanish producers of Rioja for example, use Burgundy-shaped bottles for their richer Garnacha blends whilst their more structured Tempranillo-based wines (that are meant to be aged before drinking) are put in Bordeaux-shaped bottles.

Bottle shape can also vary at the base and whilst some are flat-bottomed, others feature an indentation on the underside called a 'punt'. Traditionally this made it easier to stack bottles upside down one on top of the other (especially sparkling wine bottles). Today a punt is mostly decorative although it is useful when pouring with only one hand and is sometimes used by producers to create the impression of quality (as it increases the overall bottle width).

The weight and colour of the glass used in wine bottle manufacture varies according to producer. Heavy glass is the most expensive option (and the only one able to withstand the pressure of sparkling wine) and is used by some to imply that the wine is of a correspondingly high quality. Some producers use brown or clear glass but most use a shade of green which can range from very pale green to almost black. The colour of the bottle does not affect the quality of the wine inside it although darker shades are more suitable for wines that are meant for ageing as they reduce the amount of UV light that can penetrate through.

## ULLAGE / FILL LEVEL

Regardless of bottle shape, size or weight, the level of an everyday-drinking wine should always reach just below the bottom of the foil. If it doesn't, this is a sign that the bottle has been stored under adverse conditions and the wine has either evaporated or seeped out as a result of an excessively hot or dry environment. If the bottle does not have a foil (which is only an optional accessory), the wine should reach at least a third of the way up the neck. A certain amount of evaporation is to be expected with older vintages and this is measured in centimetres from the bottom of the cork. Fill level is the single most important factor in valuing a bottle. If the wine only reaches 'mid-shoulder' level for example, this bottle will only be worth around half its 'into-neck' counterpart whereas a bottle that displays a 'low shoulder' fill level will only be worth a nominal amount. Fill level in a champagne bottle is often measured from the bottom of the bottle when held upside down because the length of the foil may obscure the true level of the champagne. With fine old Burgundy, ullage of up to 6cm is acceptable.

## ALTERNATIVE CONTAINERS

Whilst most commercially-available wine is sold in bottle format, it can also be purchased in a box. Box containers are usually only used for everyday-drinking 'party' wines and are designed with these in mind: not only do they contain larger amounts of wine than a standard bottle (usually around 3 or 4 litres) but the wine inside also keeps for longer once opened than it would do in an opened bottle. This is because it is contained in a special bag which has an oxygen barrier and the tap used to access it is also specially-designed to prevent oxygen from entering. In Europe you can also buy wine either in or from a barrel. These contain inexpensive local wine for immediate drinking.

## CORK STOPPERS

Nearly all fine wines are stoppered with a cork. This is because it is assumed (but not proven) that fine wines that require ageing before reaching their peak need a porous stopper that allows a continuous, controlled exposure to oxygen. Cork is slowly falling out of favour however, because of the risk it carries of affecting the wine with cork taint. The quality and price of the cork minimise this risk but do not eliminate it. When choosing a mature wine you should therefore check that the cork has neither pushed up out of the bottle (if so, the foil will be raised) nor that it has fallen into the wine as a result of shrinkage (the latter is much less likely but may still occur with very old vintages). Both show that the wine has been badly stored.

Since the sealing ability of cork suffers naturally with age, some producers offer re-corking services for their finest wines (such as Penfolds in Australia and some of the top Bordeaux châteaux) – wines are first tasted to check their quality and are then topped up with wine from the same vintage before being re-sealed with a new cork.

## ALTERNATIVE STOPPERS

Increasingly winemakers are turning away from cork towards alternative stoppers, particularly for everyday-drinking wines that do not require the controlled exposure to oxygen that a cork provides. Alternative materials such as plastic (which is particularly popular in the New World) remove the risk of both cork taint and of the cork drying out. Plastic corks are also more versatile because bottles can be stored upright as well as just on their sides. The disadvantage of plastic is that it may absorb more of a wine's volatile compounds than cork and therefore adversely affect its taste. It is also less ecologically-friendly because it is not as biodegradable.

Aluminium alloy screw caps are also used to stopper bottles and offer the benefit of not requiring a corkscrew to open them. They are cheaper than cork too. Despite this, they are still not that popular because they require investment from the producer both in the form of special ridge-necked bottles and in a bottling line that can fit them.

Less common alternatives to cork include crown caps (such as those used to seal beer), corks covered in a barrier membrane to prevent potential cork taint, stoppers made of glass, and screw caps that produce a popping sound when opened (for those that are nostalgic about traditional corks).

### WINE SCORES, MEDALS & AWARDS

Measuring wine quality numerically by giving individual wines a score out of 100 is a system that was initiated by the American so-called tasting guru, Robert M Parker Jr. It has gained in popularity ever since (largely because it is so consumer-friendly) and many wine critics and specialist shops now use some sort of scoring system in order to describe their wines.

Despite its universal appeal however, it has many flaws: firstly, a wine's unique qualities cannot simply be reduced to a number, secondly, it is only a very crude way of comparing wholly different styles which cannot adequately be measured against the same yardstick. It is also a misleading system because unlike a description, a numerical score implies objectivity when in fact it is just as subjective a measure as any and depends like any other upon the scorer's individual taste. Furthermore, a score erroneously implies permanence when the qualities it is measuring are temporary – a wine evolves continuously with age after all and any assessment of it can only correspond to one particular bottle, tasted under one particular set of circumstances. Finally, it is a counterproductive scoring method because by encouraging producers to emulate the styles of wine that tend to receive the highest scores (because these can subsequently command premium prices regardless of the quality of later vintages), the measuring system itself ends up changing the very nature of what is being measured. The result is that the diversity of wine styles previously available then narrows in favour of the most commercial, homogenized examples. So whilst scores and medals can provide a very crude means of comparison between different types of wine, they should not be taken as definitive indicators of quality and should certainly not be taken too much into consideration when choosing one wine over another.

## Wine futures

Wine can be purchased at various stages in its production: either whilst the grapes are still on the vine (this is rare), whilst the wine is maturing in cask or most commonly, once it has been bottled and released onto the market. Buying from the cask is otherwise known as buying wine 'futures' or buying en primeur (from the French word 'primeur' meaning young produce). Only part of a vintage is ever sold in this way and originally it was a means for winemakers to raise capital (rather like a cash advance) before their wines were commercially released.

The most established en primeur market deals in the (mainly red, classed growth) wines of Bordeaux (encompassing its Haut Médoc, St Emilion and Pomerol regions) as well as in the sweet white dessert wines from its Sauternes region. This is for several reasons: because these wines are arguably of such consistently high quality that they are likely to remain popular with consumers, because they are only produced in very small quantities (and should therefore become more and more sought-after as their stocks diminish) and because they are amongst the wines with the longest ageing potential in the world and therefore have a long potential trading life. These wines make up the largest percentage of those traded at fine wine auction houses so their secondary market is well established. Burgundian wines on the other hand, are not as easy to trade because unlike châteaux plots, vineyards are co-owned and the quality of wines produced by them can therefore vary greatly.

## HOW IT WORKS

Sales of wine futures are based upon en primeur tastings which
are conducted exclusively for the wine trade. These are held in
Bordeaux in the spring around six months after the harvest and
wine samples are taken from the casks in which they are
maturing. Following the tasting, the wine trade make predictions
both about when these wines will be ready to drink (usually
between eight to twenty years later) as well as about their future
quality (relative to other vintages). This is challenging because
young wines taste very little like their mature counterparts – at
six months old, their fruit flavours have not yet developed fully
and both acidity and tannin levels can be unduly prominent.
Nonetheless there are certain signs that indicate potential even at
this early stage: an intense ruby-red, purple or black colour with
only a thin rim shows good fruit concentration; a firm structure
shows the wine has the potential to remain balanced as it ages; a
pronounced fruit flavour indicates that this will flesh out its
future structure; a medium to full body with aromas that develop
on the palate shows complexity and good length is an overall
sign of quality. Taking note of all these attributes in a short
period of time requires considerable stamina particularly when
there are hundreds of wines to evaluate but the greater the
number of wines that is tasted, the easier it becomes to make
quality comparisons between individual wines as well as to gauge
the general quality of the vintage as a whole.

Once the wine trade has made its predictions, merchants release
these to their clients in the form of tasting notes or scores. (These
are subjective so different merchants offer different predictions
and it is therefore advisable to compare several sets before
making a purchase). At this stage, case prices have not usually

been revealed yet and are determined later by the châteaux depending upon the reviews they receive, their perception of themselves in the regional pecking order and upon the current market price of older vintages of their wines. Châteaux will also take into consideration their need for capital as well as previous years' release prices. (Trading potential and en primeur release prices greatly increased in the 1990s, first following interest from the emerging Asian wine markets and more recently from new Russian buyers).

The next stage of the process involves merchants applying for a primary allocation of the wines they think they can sell from the châteaux's négociant representatives. But because no-one can be entirely sure of the wines' potential future quality relative to other vintages nor certain that the market will remain as keen to buy wine at a later date, their commitment carries a certain element of risk. This risk is then passed onto the client, whose gamble may or may not pay off over the course of the wine's life.

Once the châteaux have received all of the trade requests, their négociants will offer a primary allocation (called the first 'tranche' or slice) to their preferred contacts. These are the merchants with whom they have long-term relationships, those who have also in the past bought less favourably-reviewed vintages and those who have the most established reputations. Newcomers usually have to join a waiting list for the very best, most popular wines. After the first tranche has been put on the general market and offered to private investors by the trade, the châteaux may release second or third tranches to the trade, each one priced slightly higher than the last. The remainder of the stock is then sold after the wine has been bottled. In a good vintage when demand is very high, private investors can thus make considerable profits merely through selling wines bought in the first tranche either to brokers who wish to increase their allocation or to other private investors.

En primeur wine is sold in units of nine litres and private clients can a request a particular bottle format via the merchant who is buying on their behalf. Most choose either twelve 750ml bottles, six magnums containing 1,500ml each or twenty four 325ml half-bottles (the last option is more commonly requested for sweet wines that are often enjoyed in smaller quantities). The most tradable option is the first, although large format bottles are increasingly valuable not only because of their relative scarcity but also because of the inherent status symbol they represent (particularly in emerging wine markets).

En primeur prices include storage during maturation and future bottling costs. This is because the wine is only released by the châteaux one-and-a-half to two years after its purchase. They do not include tax or duty which is payable locally on receipt of the goods. Until this time the wine is described as either in or under bond and can continue to be traded without tax or duty being applied. Once it has been released by the châteaux, it can then either be stored for an annual fee with the wine merchant from whom it was purchased (most will have access to temperature, movement and light-controlled wine warehouses) or delivered directly to their clients.

## ADVANTAGES & DISADVANTAGES
The principle advantage in buying fine wines en primeur is that there may no longer be any available by the time they are ready

for drinking. Doing so also ensures that the wine has been stored under perfect conditions from the moment it is bottled until you decide to drink it (as is the case when buying any other wine under bond). Furthermore, buying en primeur can represent better value than buying the wine when it is at its peak given that the market for fine wines is increasing and its supply is fixed. Trading wine as a commodity is therefore an increasingly attractive prospect particularly in Britain where wine does not incur capital gains tax as well as in Hong Kong where wine duty has recently been abolished.

Unfortunately the growing popularity of buying wine en primeur has lead to a number of negative repercussions for the industry. As with all tastings, certain types of wines fare better than others (most commonly those that are ripe, fruity, alcoholic and rounded with relatively low tannin and acidity levels). Wines tasted en primeur however traditionally taste the opposite (they are expected to evolve into great wines rather than taste great at the time) and yet because of the press coverage and investment en primeur tastings now attract, some winemakers are deliberately producing more approachable wines at younger ages in order to receive a better rating (wines that may subsequently not stand up to the traditional lengthy maturation periods they normally undergo before reaching their peak). This is a great shame as it means that the vehicle through which the wines are sold is changing the nature of the product itself in the same way that the allure of a high wine score or medal encourages producers to create a pleasing but homogenous style.

The futures market has also encouraged some Bordeaux winemakers to become complacent: they either refuse to show their wines en primeur at all (a tactic that can either create more demand for them when bottled or which can backfire by leading critics to doubt their quality relative to others from that vintage), or they continue to increase their prices every year regardless of their wines' quality (they assume that global demand for claret will continue to grow exponentially). This is a risky long-term strategy because buyers will not necessarily remain loyal if prices are seen to be over-inflated in comparison to wines from other regions or countries, nor if there is a global financial downturn.

As a result, fine red wines from regions such as the northern Rhône (in particular those produced in its Côte Rôtie and Hermitage areas), top red and white wines from Burgundy (which make up around a fifth of all sales at fine wine auction houses), Italian 'Super Tuscans[42]' (such as Sassicaia and Tignanello) and vintage champagnes from the top Houses, all now have burgeoning en primeur markets. Wines produced in limited quantities from the New World (which usually present slightly shorter-term investments) are also joining the market, such as the 7-10,000 case a year Penfolds Grange from Australia and the Californian cult wines, Opus One and Dominus. Indeed as the number of fine wines produced in the New World continues to grow, consumers are becoming increasingly impatient with Old World wines that not only require long periods of cellaring before they reach their drinking peaks but which also seem relatively expensive in comparison as well as less approachable in style and packaging.

So whilst there are potential advantages to buying wine en primeur, it is important to bear in mind that like any investment prices may fall and that purchase prices from a particular vintage however lauded at the time, may subsequently be revealed as over-inflated upon later tastings of the same wine. Indeed great care must be taken when choosing wines for potential investment because on average only three vintages a decade are worth buying, only some Bordeaux classed growths enjoy an active secondary market and within this select group, very few usually enjoy a financial return. It is also important to consider that this market, whilst separate from and historically not as volatile as financial markets, is nonetheless linked to their rise and fall. It is therefore advisable before buying wines en primeur, to do so with a view to drinking your stocks rather than rely heavily on a potential increase in their value. You will then be pleasantly surprised if they do gain in value and will have lost nothing if they do not.

# THE TECHNICAL BIT

## WINEMAKING

*Section Three covers how grapes are made into wine, how a 'bad' vintage can be improved in the cellar, alternative types of winemaking and how to talk about wines.*

*Winemaking starts in the vineyard and both* **viticulture** *and* **vinification** *play an equal part in the process. Viticulture refers to the growth cycle of the vine and to the way in which the best possible must can be produced; vinification refers to the process that occurs once the grapes have been picked and to the way in which the best possible wine can be produced from the must.*

# The traditional method

Most still red and white wines are made according to the traditional method which has been practised in its most basic form since 5000BC.

**THE VINE**
99% of all wines are produced from grapes of the Eurasian Vitis Vinifera species. This provides the scion (or top, fruit-producing) part of the vine, which is grafted[43] onto native American, phylloxera-resistant rootstock (from species such as Vitis Riparia or Rupestris). These rootstocks are unsuitable for producing wine because their grapes display what is described as a 'foxy'[44] taste.

The practice of vine grafting came about in the 1880s after the devastation of European vineyards by the phylloxera root aphid. This was brought across from America and had a profound social and economic impact at the time, equivalent to Ireland's potato blight. Between 1860 and 1900 it killed huge amounts of Vitis Vinifera vines by attacking their roots, leading to its original name of phylloxera vastatrix or 'devastator'. In France alone, 6.2 million acres of vineyard were destroyed and had to be replanted with resistant vines, the roots of which were grafted onto fruit-producing non-resistant scions as described above.

As a general rule: the older the vine, the more complex the wine it produces. As it ages however, its yield also diminishes. Most winemakers therefore carefully balance the ages of their vines ensuring that a small percentage are over 50 years old (in many historic properties some are over 100), that a proportion are below production age (around 3 years old) and that the majority are between 3 and 35 years old, which is the optimum production age. Wines made from the youngest and oldest vines may be vinified separately either to create independent wines (a 'vielles vignes' or old vine bottling is quite common) or to be used as blending ingredients for just one principal wine (the wines from each age group contribute different elements to its overall style).

**THE VINEYARD**
Vines require a particular environment in order to produce the best possible grapes. Good vineyard drainage is crucial (through natural or artificial means) because it regulates the amount of water to which the vines are exposed and ensures that they are not water-logged: too little water is preferable to too much because a slight shortage encourages grapes to ripen and enhances fruit quality. Vineyard soil type is therefore important and light stony soils are preferable to heavy clay ones because the former provides better drainage.

Equally important is the vineyard's gradient, its distance from the surface of the water-table and the presence or absence of cover crops[45] grown between the vines. In general, vines prefer poor quality soil because this forces them to grow long roots in the search for nutrients. This in turn results in complex flavours. Fertile soil on the other hand, encourages excessive vegetation growth which results in diluted grape juice. Different grape types thrive in different soils however, and in Burgundy for example, the choice of grape variety grown by the winemaker depends upon the particular soil composition of his plot of land: Chardonnay is generally planted where limestone soils predominate and Pinot Noir is normally planted where there is more marl and clay.

The topography or surface features of a vineyard (such as its gradient, altitude, aspect and proximity to water) influence the microclimate in which a vine grows. A slight gradient is advantageous not only because it promotes better drainage than flat land but also because hillside soil tends to be poorer and therefore preferable for vine growth. A steep gradient is not ideal because not only does soil get washed down the slope in areas that receive a lot of rain but the harvest must also be done by hand which is expensive (because machines are unable to access the vines).

In a hot climate, a vineyard with a high altitude and a northerly aspect is favourable because it provides cooler growing conditions and shade from the sun whereas in a cool climate, south-facing vineyards are more sought-after. Vines that are planted on land that is close to water benefit from its moderating influence on the temperature but can suffer adversely from high levels of humidity which can lead to unwanted mildew[46].

### THE HARVEST

The harvest takes place when the grapes are mature. In the northern hemisphere, this is usually in the second half of the calendar year and in the southern hemisphere, this is usually in the first half of the calendar year. Traditionally grape maturity was assessed by measuring weight, acidity and pH level – as a grape ripens its juice becomes heavier, its acidity levels decrease and its sugar content increases. But to produce a good wine, a grape needs not only to be mature when picked but also to display ripe flavour aromas and these do not necessarily develop at the same rate as its sugar levels. In order to assess flavour maturity, a grape's phenolic ripeness must also be taken into account. This is measured by including additional physiological factors into the assessment such as skin colour, seed colour, skin texture and pulp consistency.

Harvesting by hand is the traditional method and starts with grape-pickers cutting entire bunches at the stem. If the vines are grown close to the ground so that they are both sheltered from the wind and benefit from radiated ground heat (as with the Guyot or double Guyot vine training system[47] used across much of France), this can be particularly back-breaking work! Harvest workers take care to select only predominantly healthy bunches and those that are either damaged, under-developed, shrivelled or mouldy are rejected. Healthy bunches are emptied into a tractor-trailer stationed at the end of the vineyard where they are re-checked and any unsuitable grapes are discarded. As soon as the trailer is full, it is driven to the cellar and emptied then returned to the vineyard edge to be re-filled with another load. It is important that the trailer is relatively shallow so that the bunches at the bottom are not crushed by the weight of those added on top. This would cause them to start to ferment and could result in wine with 'off' flavours.

Harvesting them by hand is a slow, labour-intensive (and therefore potentially expensive) process that can last for up to four weeks. Its advantage is that only the most healthy bunches are hand-selected for vinification whereas with a machine harvest, pre-selection is not possible. The manual method is also gentle, which is particularly important when a colourless juice is required such as when picking red grapes to make a white wine (as in the production of the base wine for champagne).

The alternative to hand-picking grapes is to harvest by machine. The principal advantage of this method is that it saves time. It is therefore preferable either if unfavourable weather conditions are on their way or if the vineyard area is very large (as is often the case in the New World). Machine harvesting also absolves the producer of following bureaucratic regulations governing the employment of a temporary workforce.

CRUSHING

The grapes are crushed as soon as they reach the cellar. Traditionally (as is still the case in some parts of Portugal) this was done by foot but nowadays it is more efficient and less expensive to use a mechanical crusher-destemmer machine. The first process involves removing the stalks of the grapes (this is done without fail in the case of white grapes and most of the time in the case of red grapes unless they are required to add extra tannins to the must). Great care is taken not to crush their pips as these can impart rancid oils and bitter tannins. After crushing, white and red wine vinification methods differ.

During white wine vinification, as soon as the grapes have been crushed and destemmed they are transferred to a grape press. The press then gently squeezes the crushed pulp in order to separate the skins from the must. Next the must is transferred to a fermentation vat, which is usually either made of an inert substance such as stainless steel or of concrete lined with inert glass or tiles. This technology is relatively new to winemaking and ensures both that the wine's delicate aromas are preserved and that the vat does not impart any flavours or qualities to it. (New Zealand's prior experience of working with stainless steel in the dairy industry played a large part in their rapid production of the clean, refreshing, quality white wines with which they are now synonymous). For particularly robust white wines, wooden fermentation vats may be used instead. These produce a rich, heady almost waxy style of wine that is capable of developing over decades. (Bordeaux's Pessac-Léognan region produces a number of superb examples such as the white wines from Domaine de Chevalier, Châteaux Haut Brion and Laville-Haut-Brion).

During red wine vinification, grape skins are kept in contact with the must and the mushy pulp is transferred directly to a fermentation vat. This is either inert or made of wood (usually oak), the latter of which independently imparts tannins as well as certain flavours to the must. The skins and possibly stalks then macerate in the must adding tannins and colour to it. Maceration times vary according to the type of wine required: to create a intensely-coloured, tannic claret it can last for up to two weeks; to make a light, fruity red wine such as France's Beaujolais it lasts only around five days; and to create a rosé wine it lasts a mere 12 to 36 hours. 'Coupage', or the blending of red and white wine to create rosé, is currently only permitted when creating rosé champagne, in the production of Spanish 'mezcla' or mixed wine (for domestic consumption only), as well as in countries outside the EU.

## FERMENTATION

Fermentation is the process during which sugar is converted into alcohol and carbon dioxide. It is such a complex process that it was only properly understood in the late 19th Century, thanks to the insights of Louis Pasteur: during his studies of wine, he noted that fermentation was not spontaneous (as was commonly assumed) but instead a result of yeasts feeding upon grape sugars. He observed that unattended grapes naturally ferment into wine as soon as their skin has been broken. This is due to the action of wild yeasts naturally present on their 'bloom' (the whitish film of wax found on their skins). Acetobacter bacteria also present on the bloom then cause the wine to ferment. This process continues until the wine eventually turns into vinegar.

Wild yeasts are not only found on grape skins but also on the equipment and in the ambient atmosphere of a wine cellar so fermentation begins almost as soon as the grapes have been crushed. Wild yeasts are unreliable however, and fermentation may either stall before all of the grape sugar has been consumed (described as a 'stuck fermentation' which results in an unstable wine) or they may produce wine with an off flavour. As a result, most New World producers (along with increasing numbers of Old World producers) prefer to use more predictable, cultured yeasts instead. This means killing the wild yeasts whilst the grapes are being crushed through the addition of sulphur dioxide[48]. Many traditional producers nonetheless prefer to rely on unpredictable wild yeasts and continue to take the associated winemaking risks, insisting that it is the unique mix of wild yeasts that is found in their cellar that contributes to their particular style of wine.

During a controlled, commercial fermentation, one of over a hundred different strains of cultured yeast is introduced. Each strain has different properties and is chosen according to both the type of grapes being fermented and the style of wine desired: it may be especially sulphur dioxide-, alcohol-, or temperature-tolerant; it may ferment the grapes either more quickly or more slowly than usual; or it may impart a particular flavour[49] to the resulting wine. The winemaker therefore chooses a yeast that best suits his needs – in some New World wine regions for example where over-ripe grapes with high sugar levels are vinified, alcohol-tolerant yeasts are essential; in a small cellar with only a few fermentation tanks available, speed may instead be of the essence.

As well as producing carbon dioxide, fermentation also produces heat. This helps to speed up the process but can also have a detrimental effect if it is allowed to rise uncontrollably: yeasts may die (this usually happens at around 40°C), off flavours may develop, desirable flavours may be destroyed, harmful bacteria such as acetobacter may be encouraged to grow, and the wine may start to oxidise and turn brown.

Ideal fermentation temperatures vary across winemaking regions and grape varieties but white wine is generally fermented at relatively low temperatures (between 12-20°C) because heat adversely affects its delicate aromas. The process usually lasts between several weeks to several months and temperatures are kept low by running cold water over the outsides of the fermentation vats (stainless steel ones are fitted with electronic thermometers and cooling equipment).

Red wine fermentation usually lasts between four days to a week and takes place at higher temperatures (between 25-30°C). This is because heat is required to maximise the extraction of colour, flavour compounds and tannins from the grape skins and possibly stalks into the naturally colourless grape juice. In order to distribute these evenly and prevent the skins floating to the top of the vat, 'pumping over' regularly takes place. This means wine is drawn off the bottom of the vat and is pumped back through the crust at the top, which also serves to aerate the wine providing it with the oxygen it needs to continue to ferment.

RACKING & PRESSING

When fermentation has stopped the resulting wine is racked, which means it is drawn off its lees (the mush of mainly dead yeast cells that have gravitated to the bottom of the fermentation vat). Most white wines are then transferred either to new vats or to wooden casks where they spend some time maturing. Some however, are either not racked at all or they are racked a few days later so that they gain the fullness of body and the slightly yeasty, creamy flavours that an extended period of contact with their lees imparts.

During red wine vinification, the first batch to be racked is called 'free-run' wine, which is about 70% of the total available grape juice. (Different grape varieties give different yields but as a general rule: one kilogram of grapes produces one 750ml bottle of wine). The free-run wine is then transferred either to new vats or to wooden casks in order to mature whilst the remaining lees are gently pressed to create 'press' wine. This is more tannic and structured than free-run wine and the two may either be matured and bottled separately as the free-run premium and press wine second label wines of a single property or the press wine may be used as a blending ingredient in the base, free-run wine. Sometimes a second pressing of the lees takes place which produces a rustic wine with high tannins. The remaining lees of both white and red wines are then either discarded or used as fertiliser.

MATURATION

Superior quality white and red wines usually undergo a prolonged maturation period because their flavours are likely to develop and gain in complexity during this time. This is reflected in their premium price (maturation requires additional investment from the winemaker in wooden maturation barrels or casks as well as in additional cellar space). Everyday-drinking wines on the other hand, are not likely to develop much in complexity as they mature so they are usually bottled young and released immediately.

The length of time a wine spends maturing depends upon the quality of the vintage, the style of wine desired and upon domestic wine regulations. Most fine red wines are matured in wooden casks for eighteen to twenty four months during which they are regularly racked off their lees. Like wooden fermentation vats, casks impart certain flavours and tannins to a wine, deepen its colour and provide ideal conditions for its slow, natural 'clarification' (during which any remaining lees fall slowly to the bottom of the vessel). Wooden casks also allow a wine's flavours to develop through a gradual process of evaporation and absorption. They therefore need to be topped up frequently with wine from other casks in order to ensure that the wine does not become oxidised through over-exposure to air.

The precise nature of the wooden cask in which the wine is matured plays an important role in its resulting style. Usually they are made of either American or French oak and the winemaker will choose the exact provenance of the wood according to its tannin levels, sap levels and type of grain, which varies from forest to forest. The way the wood has been cut (whether it has been either sawn or hand split) is also important, as is the level to which the wood has been toasted whilst being shaped into a barrel: wood that has been lightly-toasted imparts lots of tannins as well as oaky, woody and vegetal aromas, whereas wood that has received a heavy toast imparts spicy aromas and less tannins (the toast acts as a barrier between the wine and the barrel).

The age of the cask is significant too. New casks have the most concentrated effect and are therefore the most expensive. They are used for only the most robust wines which have sufficiently concentrated fruit levels not to be overpowered by them. As a cask ages its effect on a wine diminishes and by the time it is around four years old, it imparts almost no tannins nor flavour. The winemaker therefore varies the exposure of his wines to wood by either maturing different batches of the same vintage in different types of wood before blending them, or by limiting the time his wines spend in new wood before they are transferred to older barrels to continue their maturation.

### FINING, STABILISATION & FILTRATION
As a wine matures, it precipitates deposits made up of dead yeast cells, tannins and proteins (hence red wines lose their colour and tannins and throw a sediment as they get older). Larger particles naturally fall to the bottom of the cask during vinification but smaller particles often remain suspended in solution. These are beneficial to a fine wine (they contribute to its aroma and colour, and also enhance its ageing capacity) but their presence also carries risks. If they are not removed before the wine is bottled it is not as heat stable and may become cloudy or develop an unpleasant taste at a later date.

Most wines are therefore clarified or 'fined' during the vinification process, either just once (in the case of fine wines) or several times (in the case of everyday-drinking wines). This involves stirring a fining agent such as gelatine, bentonite or white of egg into the wine to attract the suspended particles. These coagulate and then gravitate to the bottom of the vat where they are discarded when the wine is racked.

Next the wine may undergo further stabilising processes such as the addition of sulphur dioxide, refrigeration or flash heating. This prevents microbiological and chemical problems from arising after the wine has been bottled (including unwanted deposits, gas, cloudiness or the presence of bacteria which could cause either a bad smell, an oily texture, loss of colour or bitterness).

Filtering a wine is another means of making it clear and bright. A rough filtration removes any large particles and a more thorough filtration takes place at the final stage of vinification. This involves straining the wine through a filter that is small enough to catch potentially harmful yeasts and bacteria. Cask maturation has a stabilising effect on wine so fine red wines only undergo a very gentle filtration, if any. A final filtration may take place after all the casks have been blended so as to avoid potential bottle variation.

## BOTTLING

Bottling is the final stage of the vinification process. Most winemakers use a mobile bottling line but because this is usually shared (and therefore not always available when needed), an increasing number of high quality wine producers are investing in their own machines.

Once the wine has been decanted into a bottle, it is sealed with a stopper, a foil is added (which is optional except for French wines for sale in France which require a customs seal on top), and a label is put on. It is important that the stabilised wine is not contaminated during this process either by the air, the stopper or the bottling equipment.

## Modified vinification

If grapes are either harvested before they have reached their optimum ripeness or if they have been adversely affected by rot or frost, their must may result in an unbalanced wine. There are a number of ways in which the must can be modified to prevent this although the method that is used depends upon what is permitted in each winemaking region.

### CHAPTALISATION / ENRICHMENT

If grapes struggle to ripen either because of cool summer temperatures or insufficient sunlight during their growth cycle, they will display low sugar levels and high levels of acidity. This produces must that is dilute and lacking in fruit concentration. To create balance, it can be chaptalised prior to fermentation with the addition of either sugar or concentrated grape must (euphemistically the French term is 'improved'). When the yeasts are introduced there is thus more sugar for them to feed off, which results in a wine with a fuller body and a higher final alcohol level than would have been produced naturally. Chaptalisation is common in cool-climate, wine-producing countries such as Germany and the United Kingdom. In France's Bordeaux and Burgundy regions, it is forbidden to both enrich and acidify the same must.

### DEACIDIFICATION

Another means of creating balance in a low sugar, high acidity must is to deacidify it. Deacidification is common in Germany, the United Kingdom, Canada and New Zealand's South Island. Unlike chaptalisation, it usually takes place after fermentation.

There are several ways to deacidify must: it can either be diluted with water (a method that is usually accompanied by chaptalisation) or chemicals that react to and precipitate the acids can be added so that they can then be filtered out of solution. (A commonly-used additive is calcium carbonate, more commonly known as chalk).

Deacidification also occurs when wine undergoes a malolactic fermentation. Even though this process is called fermentation (perhaps because like fermentation it also produces carbon dioxide), it is actually merely a conversion by lactic bacteria of the harsh malic acids in wine to softer lactic acids. The advantage of deacidifying a wine in this way is that malolactic fermentation also contributes complexity to the resulting wine and prevents an uncontrolled fermentation from occurring after it has been bottled (which could lead to unwanted bubbles.) The disadvantage is that it needs to be rigorously controlled otherwise it may produce overpowering buttery aromas. It can also strip a wine of too much acidity and make it flabby so that ironically, it then needs to be re-acidified.

## ACIDIFICATION

In hot-climate regions grapes may quickly become overripe resulting in must that is flabby and lacking in structure. This may be acidified to create balance but the difficulty lies in gauging exactly how much acid is required to produce the desired pH level. The most common additives are tartaric and malic acids because citric acid, which is the cheapest option is forbidden in the EU. These are usually added before or during fermentation although they may also be added just before the wine is bottled.

## CONCENTRATION

If either a lot of rain has fallen during the grape's growing cycle (so that the vineyard is water-logged) or if the grapes are picked before they have reached phenolic ripeness, they may produce a dilute and watery must. To create balance, the excess water can be drawn out through concentration. (Usually only a small proportion of the total grape must is modified in this way as the process may also remove flavour compounds). This is done by evaporating water off the must under either low pressure conditions or a vacuum so that its boiling point is reduced to around 20°C. Since this is the same temperature as fermentation, there is minimal risk of flavour loss.

Wine can also be concentrated through reverse osmosis. This entails drawing the excess water out of the wine (towards a solution with a higher concentration) through a partially permeable filter that only lets small water molecules through.

# Other types of wine

As wine drinkers become both more health-conscious and environmentally-aware, the market for alternative types of wine that respond to these new demands is growing.

## DEALCOHOLISED & REDUCED ALCOHOL WINE

Dealcoholised and reduced alcohol wines are vinified in the traditional method except most of their alcohol content is removed before they are bottled. They are thus both less calorific (they have only around 150 calories per standard bottle) and also cheaper than normal wines (there is less duty payable on them). 'No alcohol' wines contain less than 2% alcohol and if there remains between 2 and 5.5% alcohol, they are classified as 'low alcohol' or 'reduced alcohol' wine.

Alcohol can be removed in several ways: it can either be evaporated off, drawn off through osmosis, the wine can be diluted with water or fruit juice to make a type of spritzer, or fermentation of the grape must can be halted prematurely (which is a similar method to that which is used in the creation of certain types of sweet wine). Unfortunately most methods also strip the wine of its characteristic flavour and unlike dealcoholised beer which can taste convincingly authentic, dealcoholised wine tastes more like artificial fruit juice than traditional wine.

## VEGETARIAN & VEGAN WINE

Producers of vegetarian and vegan wines avoid using animal-based products during vinification. Since the most commonly-used stabilising and fining agents are animal-based, bentonite (which is a form of clay) is used instead.

## SUSTAINABLE, ORGANIC & BIODYNAMIC PRACTICES

Sustainable viticulture aims to minimise degradation to the environment by promoting both an organic approach to vineyard management as well as the use of renewable energy. Currently the EU only has the guidelines in place to certify organic vineyard practices (around 2% of the world's vineyards are registered as organic). These stipulate that everything that comes into contact with the vine (such as fertilizers and pesticides) must be natural and neither chemically-altered nor genetically modified. Most wines are unable to call themselves entirely organic however, firstly because there are no EU guidelines yet concerning organic vinification and secondly, because these would specify that everything that came into contact with the grape juice in the cellar must also be entirely natural. Since most wines are stabilised with non-organic sulphur dioxides, the nearest a wine can currently get to being described as organic is thus to be classified as 'wine made from organically-grown grapes' (or 'vin biologique' in France).

Biodynamic viticulture is the greenest form of sustainable viticulture because it advocates the use of organic products as well as sustainable, natural practices (such as the use of horses instead of tractors). Its methods are what detractors would describe as mystically-inclined however because they also follow the biodynamic calendar, which is heavily influenced by the zodiac.

The concept is based on the writings of Rudolph Steiner who argued that plants were not just material things but also spiritual beings. He felt that they should be viewed in a wider context than just a biological one and that the solar, lunar, planetary and stellar cycles actually influenced plant growth according to their position in the zodiac. His claim was thus that food quality would be enhanced if pruning, spraying and harvesting were carried out at the appropriate moment in the earth's cosmic and particularly lunar cycle.

According to biodynamic viticulture, a vine has four parts (roots, leaves/shoots, flowers and grapes) each of which is linked to one of the four elements (earth, water, air and fire). It therefore encourages the tending of a vine's roots for example (which are the part that represents the earth) only when the moon is in one of the zodiac's earth signs (Taurus, Virgo or Capricorn).

Sceptics argue that these methods are irrational and based more on magic than science but French government research has found that biodynamic soils and the roots of the vines grown in them, do indeed show higher levels of microbial life than those of conventional vineyards. Because there are so few biodynamic wines to analyse however and to do so properly would require comparing both a biodynamic and a conventional wine produced from the same vineyard, it is hard to prove whether it is the biodynamic practices in particular that create a quality wine or whether this is merely a result of the inherent skill of its winemakers – most biodynamic wines also happen to be produced by top-quality winemakers such as Chapoutier from the Rhône Valley, Domaine Leflaive in Burgundy and Pingus from Spain's Ribera del Duero region.

## TALKING ABOUT WINE

*Now that you have the knowledge, you need the vocabulary!
The following user-guide takes a look at the often-confusing
technical and descriptive terms that surround the subject of wine.*

## A glossary of winespeak

### DESCRIBING WINES

| | |
|---|---|
| ACIDIC | makes your mouth water. This is usually a refreshing sensation but if the wine is overly acidic and lacking in balance, it can be seen as a fault. |
| AROMA | a pleasant smell (as opposed to an unpleasant 'odour'). |
| ASTRINGENT | seems to shrivel the skin of your mouth. |
| ATTACK | the initial impression of a wine soon after it enters your mouth. |
| BIG | full-bodied (this usually also means that the wine is high in alcohol). |
| BODY | gives a sense of 'weight' in your mouth – can be described as light, medium or full. |
| BOTTLE SICKNESS | a movement-induced wine fault that results in unclean aromas. |
| BOUQUET | the combination of aromas found in a mature, complex wine. |
| CLOSED | non-descript and lacking in aromas, either on the nose and/or palate. (Usually only a temporary phase). |
| CLOYING | sickly sweet; full-bodied but lacking in balancing acidity. |
| CORKED | either smells and/or tastes of dusty old books and mould with no fresh fruit aromas. |
| CORK TAINT | found in 5% of all corks and responsible for producing corky aromas in the smell and/or taste of a wine. Caused by a reaction in the fungi naturally present in cork which then produce 2,4,6-trichloroanisole (TCA). |
| CRISP | refreshing; the wine's acidity is balanced by its fruit and structure. |
| DRY | technically this means that a wine has less than 2 grammes/litre of residual sugar although it is also used to describe one that doesn't taste sweet. A wine that is off-dry tastes slightly sweet. |

| | |
|---|---|
| FAT | full-bodied; can also be used pejoratively to mean flabby. |
| FINISH | the final impression of a wine after you have either swallowed or spat it out. |
| FLABBY | a wine that is lacking in acidity and feels the opposite of refreshing. |
| FOXY | musky – smelling and tasting like a wet, cheap fur coat. Used to describe the wines produced by phylloxera-resistant native American vines. |
| LENGTH | the amount of time you are able to taste the wine after you have either swallowed or spat it out. |
| MADERISED | smells and tastes either of sherry or of madeira rather than of fresh fruit. |
| MOUTHFEEL | the impression of a wine created by its texture and body. |
| MUSTY | smells neither of fruit nor fresh but old and dusty. |
| NOSE | the smell, aroma or bouquet of a wine. |
| NOTES | aromas. |
| ONE-DIMENSIONAL | does not develop on the palate and seems lacking in complexity, thin, unstructured and even watery. |
| OXIDISED | smells and tastes of stewed or cooked rather than of fresh fruit. |
| PALATE | the tasting capability of the mouth. Employed when describing the impression of a wine for example "peachy aromas on the palate". |
| ROUNDED | medium to full-bodied and balanced (its acids, tannins and fruit concentration are in harmony). |
| STRUCTURED | a wine that shows concentrated fruit as well as high levels of tannins and acidity (it feels the opposite of flabby). |
| THICK | when referring to white wines: flabby (or full-bodied but lacking in balancing acidity and complexity); when referring to red wines: overly tannic and lacking in acidity. |

THIN                one-dimensional and lacking in fruit concentration, structure and body.

UMAMI               Japanese term for the fifth primary taste that can be translated as meaning both essence and delicious.

VARIETAL            the concept behind the production of a wine that is
CORRECTNESS         'typical' of its grape variety and extols its unique characteristics rather than hides them in order to create a more commercial, but homogenous 'incorrect' style.

VISCOSITY           the quality of being resistant to movement in the mouth which results in an impression of fullness of body (more easily noticeable in high-alcohol, sweet wines).

---

# TECHNICAL TERMS

AÉRIENNE            rather intangible French concept (meaning both ethereal and skybound), which refers to the unique conditions enjoyed by a specific plot of land in conjunction with its terroir.

ALDEHYDES           chemical compounds that enhance a wine's flavour which are formed when alcohol is exposed to air.

ASPECT              the direction in which a hill slope faces (important in terms of defining how much sunlight a vineyard receives).

BLOOM               the whitish film on the skin of a grape that helps guard against spores and loss of moisture.

CHAPTALISATION      the addition of sugar to unfermented grape must either
/ ENRICHMENT        before or during fermentation in order to increase the alcoholic content of the final wine. Only practised in Northern Europe where grapes may struggle to ripen.

CULTURED            relatively predictable group of yeasts of which only one
YEAST               strain is usually used to start a controlled fermentation of grape must. Unlike wild yeasts, these are unlikely either to produce off aromas or to cease to work mid-fermentation.

FLAVONOIDS — the most prevalent phenolic compounds that are found in wine which contribute to its colour, bitterness and texture. Since they are present in particular in a grape's stems, skins and seeds, they are thus found in higher doses in red wines than in white (because grape skins are macerated with the must during red wine production). They are thought to have an antioxidant and cancer chemopreventive effect.

FREE-RUN JUICE — produced by the sheer weight of the grapes put into both transportation vehicles and fermentation vessels prior to their being pressed. The more delicate free-run juice is usually drawn off and put into a separate tank into which the sturdier press juice is added before a blend of the two is fermented. Some fine white wines are made uniquely from free-run juice.

GREY ROT — harmful form of botrytis fungus that occurs under excessively humid conditions. If it affects dark-skinned, unripe or damaged grapes, it produces off flavours in the resulting wines.

LEES — the mush of mainly dead yeast cells, bits of grape pulp, skins, stems and seeds that gravitates to the bottom of the barrel during fermentation. Some wines are deliberately left in contact with their lees to acquire a specific flavour and to gain in complexity (such as the base wines that are later made into champagne and some French Muscadet wines).

MALOLACTIC FERMENTATION (MLF) — the conversion of the harsh malic acids present in new wines to softer lactic acids and carbon dioxide. The conversion (rather than fermentation) is achieved by lactic acid bacteria naturally present in most wineries.

MUST — mixture of grape pulp, juice, seeds (and in the case of red wine, skins and possibly stems) that is the result of the first crush after the harvest.

NOBLE GRAPE VARIETY — one that grows successfully and has the potential to produce quality wines in many types of climate and terroir, for example Chardonnay or Cabernet Sauvignon.

NOBLE ROT — desired type of botrytis fungus (when making sweet wine) that only occurs under particular climatic conditions. When it affects healthy, ripe, white grapes, the result is a highly complex sweet wine. Also referred to as just 'botrytis'.

PHENOLIC COMPOUNDS — chemicals that are found in grapes (particularly in their stems, skins and seeds) which multiply with exposure to the sun. They are either non-flavonoid or flavonoid and are thought to contribute to a reduced risk of heart disease.

PHENOLIC RIPENESS — fashionable concept (particularly in the New World) that refers to an alternative measure of grape ripeness which also takes into account its skin and seed colour as well as its texture, as opposed to just its weight, acidity and pH level. The distinction is important in hot-climate regions where grapes can quickly reach analytical ripeness (by registering high sugar levels) and yet lack complexity of flavour.

PHYLLOXERA — root aphid imported from America that wreaked havoc on 19th Century European vines and destroyed 6.2 million acres of vineyard in France alone.

PRESS JUICE — juice produced as a result of pressing grapes which varies in style depending upon the type of press used and the pressure exerted by it: some presses can be adjusted to exert only a very gentle force and therefore produce must that is not dissimilar to free-run juice (such as the horizontal press that squeezes grapes against the side of the machine with an expandable airbag) others produce wine that is astringent and bitter (such as the cheapest, continuous screw presses used in some large-scale, commercial wineries). Press juice is used either as a blending ingredient in a first wine or as the principal component of a second or third label wine (often the last is not commercially-available but is provided either with lunch or in lieu of payment for harvest grape pickers).

PUMPING OVER  a method of maximising contact between the fermenting grape juice and its skins, stems and pips (which impart colour and tannins) by means of drawing wine off the bottom of the fermentation vessel and pumping it back through the top of the vat thereby breaking the crust or 'cap' they form on its surface. This process also serves to aerate the fermenting juice (the yeasts responsible for fermentation need oxygen in order to grow).

RACKING  removing sediment from a wine (usually made up of its lees) by drawing the wine off one vessel and transferring it into a clean one. Racking takes place several times before a wine is bottled: firstly just after fermentation and then several times during the colder months to remove any tartrates that may have precipitated out of solution. The process also aerates the wine.

RESIDUAL SUGAR  sugar that remains once the fermentation of grape must has stopped. Amounts vary and range from 1 gramme/litre (the minimum present in most wines) to 25 grammes/litre. If a wine has less than 2 grammes/litre it is referred to as 'dry'.

RESVERATROL  a non-flavonoid compound that is produced by grape skins and which is thus found in higher concentrations in red wines (and in particular, red Burgundy) than in white wines. It is thought to have both a cancer chemopreventive effect and also to confer other beneficial health effects such as reducing platelet clumps and liver lipids.

STABILISATION  winemaking process that takes place prior to bottling which includes the addition of sulphur dioxide (to prevent unwanted microbiological changes) and a combination of refrigeration, filtration and fining to prevent subsequent chemical or physical changes occurring such as unwanted deposits or haze.

SULPHUR DIOXIDE  commonly used in the vineyard (to feed the vine as well as prevent powdery mildew) and in the cellar both as a preservative (it prevents oxidation) and also a killer of bacteria and wild yeasts which might impede a controlled fermentation and produce off flavours. The amount that can be added to wine is regulated because it can produce unpleasant aromas (the palate is quite sensitive to its presence, particularly in acidic white wines – too much sulphur and a wine can smell similar to one that is corked).

TARTRATES crystalline deposits that are found both in wine lees and also on the sides of fermentation vessels which are made up of dead yeast cells, grape pulp and tannins. These may precipitate out of solution once the wine has been bottled and although they are harmless, most producers prefer to filter wines before bottling them in order to prevent this occurring.

TERROIR French term for the concept that the unique, natural environment of a particular plot of land (including its soil type, geology, drainage, topography and microclimate) produces a unique style of wine independently of the skill of the winemaker.

TOAST heat to which a barrel is exposed as part of its manufacture which can be light, medium or heavy. The degree to which a barrel is toasted influences the amount of flavour and tannin that is imparted to the wine that is either matured or fermented in it: a heavy toast imparts pronounced spicy flavours (such as ginger, cloves, smoked meats and toasted bread) but not much tannin (the toast acts as a barrier between the wine and the wood); whereas a medium toast allows more woody, oaky and vegetal flavours through from the barrel and imparts subtle aromas of vanilla and coffee.

TOPOGRAPHY the geographical features of an area including its gradient, altitude, aspect and proximity to water.

VANILLIN an aldehyde which contributes to the vanilla flavour that is present in the vanilla bean as well as in some types of grape and also in oak. This is the reason that some wines are matured in new oak barrels.

VINTAGE the year in which the grapes are harvested. Judged as 'good' or 'bad' in a particular area according to the weather during that growing season. (It is important to bear in mind that the quality of the wine produced that year is just as reliant upon the terroir of a particular plot and the winemaker's expertise as it is upon vintage).

VITIS VINIFERA Euroasian vine species that produces the scion which is grafted onto phylloxera-resistant native American rootstock.

| VOLATILE ACIDITY | in low doses, volatile acidity (most commonly acetic acid) lifts a wine and adds complexity and fruitiness. In higher doses (above 1.5 grammes/litre), the reaction between it and the alcohol in a wine produces a vinegary flavour. A big-bodied, tannic, alcoholic wine can support a reasonably high level of acetic acid without tasting out-of-balance. |
| --- | --- |
| WILD YEAST | group of yeasts found naturally on grape skins that cause fermentation to start once these are broken. They are normally killed at the start of fermentation (by the addition of sulphur dioxide) so that cultured yeasts can take over instead (wild yeasts are unreliable and stop functioning when the fermenting must reaches around 5% alcohol). |

◆ ── ◆

## WINE TRADE TERMS

| AGENCY | the exclusive right to sell a particular wine both wholesale and/or retail in a specified geographical area. |
| --- | --- |
| BOTTLE SHAPE | a wine bottle is referred to anatomically and possesses shoulders, a lip (both of which vary in width) and a neck (which can vary in width and length). Its shoulders and neck are used to describe fill levels. |
| BOTTLE VARIATION | term that refers to usually subtle but sometimes marked variations in quality and taste between bottles from the same vineyard and vintage. These may be the result of different storage conditions, maturation rates or bottling batches (in the case of wines that are not blended prior to bottling). |
| CO-OPERATIVE | a wine business that is owned by a number of different (usually small) producers so that they may benefit from communal (and therefore cheaper) equipment and marketing costs as well as from EU subsidies. |

| | |
|---|---|
| DUTY PAID | the status of a wine once it has been taken out of bond and has incurred duty. Charges vary (they are usually lower in wine-producing countries than in non-wine producing countries) and may be applied twice when exporting wines abroad (once on release, once upon arrival). Duty is either applied as a flat rate per litre (which is beneficial to consumers of expensive fine wines) or as a percentage of the wine's cost price. |
| EN PRIMEUR | the method of buying wine 'futures' traditionally only offered by the finest châteaux in Bordeaux in order to ease their cash flow. Now also increasingly offered by other small producers of fine wine to satisfy the growing demand for alternative, potential investment opportunities. |
| FOIL/CAPSULE | the optional metallic, plastic or tin cover to the cork which acts as a further seal. |
| IN/UNDER BOND | the status in which en primeur or new wines are first released by châteaux and under which duty charges can be deferred. This makes the trading and possible import and export of cases more straightforward. Once a wine has incurred duty it can no longer go back into bond. |
| LEFT BANK | south bank of Bordeaux's Gironde estuary (into which both the Garonne and Dordogne rivers flow). The mainly red wine regions of the Médoc, Graves and Pessac-Léognan are located on this side of the estuary (and river Garonne further south) as are the sweet white wine districts of Sauternes and Barsac. The dominant grape variety in most of the left bank's red wine blends is Cabernet Sauvignon. |
| MICROCHÂTEAUX | right bank properties that produce very small quantities of wine (only several hundred cases per vintage) in a forward, oaky, very fruity style, similar to that of New World fine wines. They became a phenomenon as interest in wine speculation grew in the 1990s and their prices rose exponentially. Demand has since waned for most apart from Le Pin. |

NÉGOCIANT     a type of wine merchant that buys either grapes, must or wines from smaller producers and blends them to sell under his own brand. Some also own vineyards. Négociants are more common in areas where vineyard holdings are small such as in Burgundy.

NEW WORLD     a term that originally referred to the new colonies established as a result of European (or Old World) exploration. Winemaking is a more recent concept here than in the Old World and technology (rather than tradition) is paramount. New World wines are distinguished by the fact that they are usually categorised both by the grape varieties in their blend as well as by geographical provenance. Nowadays however, differences between Old World and New World wines are decreasing as winemaking techniques and traditional practices are shared.

OENOLOGY     the study of wine (derived from the ancient Greek for wine 'oinos'). The term has evolved to mean the more technical scientific study of winemaking and lately viticulture too. Many wineries employ consultant oenologists to confer skills and as a result cachet to their brands.

OLD WORLD     a term that refers to countries that have an established winemaking history that dates back centuries (mainly Europe and other Mediterranean countries such as North Africa and the Near East). Old World wines are usually categorised according to their geographical provenance alone and are produced according to strict winemaking specifications which follow traditional practices. Terroir is an important Old World concept.

PUNT     optional indentation in the bottom of a bottle which is useful when pouring with one hand.

QUALITY WINE     one that has met the requirements of the EU Quality Wine category and has been produced in a specific geographical region according to its particular wine regulations. Wines that do not qualify are classified as Table Wine.

RIGHT BANK — the north bank of the river Dordogne where a number of lesser wine districts as well as St. Emilion and Pomerol are located. The predominant grape varieties in most of its red wine blends are Merlot and Cabernet Franc. Located in between the two Gironde tributaries (and therefore between the left and right banks), lies the Entre-deux-Mers or 'between two seas' district which produces mainly everyday-drinking white wines.

SPITOON — vessel provided at professional tastings into which people may choose to spit wine instead of swallowing it to avoid the effects of alcohol.

SUPER SECONDS — term that refers to a few of Bordeaux's left-bank châteaux whose wines are regularly considered to be of first growth quality even though they are not officially classified as such. These are: Châteaux Pichon-Longueville-Lalande, Pichon Longueville (Baron), Cos d'Estournel, Montrose, Léoville Las Cases, Ducru-Beaucaillou, Palmer and La-Mission-Haut Brion.

SUPER TUSCAN — innovative wines (produced in Italy since the 1970s such as Sassicaia and Tignanello) whose winemakers chose to ignore traditional winemaking regulations. As a result their wines qualified only for Table Wine status despite their quality and premium price.

TROPHY WINES — those distinguished by their fame and most notably price (which is often linked to a high score from the wine critic, Robert Parker) even though this is not necessarily a reflection of their intrinsic quality but more a reflection of their 'limited edition' status and of the strength of their marketing department.

ULLAGE — the space found in either a barrel or a bottle that is not occupied by wine. When referring to a barrel, ullage also means the process of evaporation that leads to that space; when referring to a bottle, the ullage is also known as the fill level. Ullage is a good indicator of past storage history especially when buying second-hand wines (such as at auction): the larger the space, the greater the risk of oxidation although it is important to bear the length of the cork in mind too (Château Mouton Rothschild now uses shorter-than-standard corks in order to reduce the amount of wine they absorb).

# ENDNOTES

[1]  the year in which its grapes were harvested. This is shown on the bottle label and cork and is judged 'good' or 'bad' in a particular area according to the weather during that growing season.

[2]  desired type of fungus also known as botrytis that only occurs under specific climatic conditions. When it affects healthy, ripe, white grapes, the result is a highly complex sweet wine.

[3]  a term that originally referred to the new colonies established as a result of European (or Old World) exploration. Winemaking is a more recent concept here than in the Old World and technology (rather than tradition) is paramount. New World wines are distinguished by the fact that they are usually categorised both by the grape varieties in their blend as well as by their geographical provenance. Nowadays however, differences between Old World and New World wines are decreasing as winemaking techniques and traditional practices are shared.

[4]  sugar that remains once the fermentation of grape juice has stopped. Amounts range from 1 gram per litre (the minimum present in most wines) to 25 grammes per litre. If a wine has less than 2 grammes per litre it will taste dry.

[5]  non-descript and lacking in aromas.

[6]  the amount of time you are able to taste a wine after you have swallowed or spat it out.

[7]  its acid levels, tannin levels, alcohol and fruit concentration are in all harmony.

[8]  the conversion of harsh malic acids present in young wines to softer lactic acids and carbon dioxide. The conversion (rather than fermentation) is achieved by lactic acid bacteria naturally present in most wineries.

[9]  the removal of excess water from a wine during its vinification process by means of either evaporation or reverse osmosis.

[10]  abbreviation of ethyl alcohol – the colourless, odourless substance usually referred to as alcohol.

[11]  heat to which a barrel is exposed as part of its manufacture. The toast can be light, medium or heavy depending upon the temperature and length of time a barrel is exposed to it. The toast will affect different kinds of oak in different ways but with all types of wood, the degree of toast affects the style of wine matured or fermented in it by imparting different flavours and

levels of tannins: a heavy toast imparts pronounced spicy flavours such as ginger, cloves, smoked meats and toasted bread but does not impart much tannin because the toast acts as a barrier between the wine and the wood; a medium toast allows more woody, oaky and vegetal flavours through from the barrel and gives a wine subtle vanilla and coffee aromas.

12   see Section Two, Enjoying Wine, Wine Faults.

13   whether a wine is a true reflection of the grape varieties in its blend or not: a wine should be vinified in a way that highlights the unique characteristics of its grape varieties rather than in a way that masks these in favour of a possibly more commercially-successful style. Varietal correctness should form part of your quality assessment.

14   those you are most likely to come across as single variety wines either for sale in a wine shop or on a restaurant list.

15   when a grape's characteristics vary significantly according to where it is grown, the wines it produces are described twice according to whether they were produced either in a hot-climate country or in a cool-climate country.

16   the most important areas to produce quality examples of that grape as well as those you are most likely to see for sale.

17   an area that starts in Dijon and stretches south towards Cheilly lès Maranges. It encompasses both the Côte de Nuits region in the north, where most of the region's finest red wines are produced and the Côte de Beaune region in the south, where most of the region's finest dry white wines are produced.

18   refers mainly to Europe and other Mediterranean countries such as North Africa and the Near East which have an established winemaking history that dates back centuries. Wines from Old World countries are usually categorised according to their geographical provenance alone and are made to strict winemaking specifications which take in traditional practices. Terroir is a key factor here.

19   the direction in which the slope of a hill faces (important in terms of defining the amount of sunlight the vineyard receives).

20   wines that share the name of the grape that is either their only ingredient or the dominant variety in their blend (constituting over 75%).

21   the south bank of Bordeaux's Gironde estuary into which both the Garonne and Dordogne rivers flow. The mainly red wine regions of the Médoc, Graves and Pessac-Léognan are located on this side of the estuary as are the sweet white wine districts of Sauternes and Barsac. Cabernet Sauvignon is the dominant grape variety in most of the left bank's red wine blends.

[22] the north bank of the Gironde estuary where a number of lesser wine districts as well as St. Emilion and Pomerol are located. Merlot and Cabernet Franc are the predominant grape varieties in most of the right bank's red wine blends.

[23] properties located on Bordeaux's right bank that produce very small quantities of wine (only several hundred cases per vintage) in a forward, oaky, very fruity style similar to that of New World fine wines. They gained notoriety in the 1990s as interest in wine speculation grew and their prices rose exponentially. (Demand has since waned for most apart from Le Pin).

[24] these are more likely to form part of a blend than to form single variety wines.

[25] those whose wines you are most likely to come across either for sale in a shop or on a restaurant list. New World wine regions are not described because wines from these areas are almost always labelled according to their grape variety.

[26] indicates that the region is best known for its red wines.

[27] in 1855 the red wines of Bordeaux were classified according to their current market price and those that qualified for classed growth status (the 'crus classés') were divided up into five ranks. Originally four châteaux were given the highest accolade of first growth and Château Mouton Rothschild joined their ranks in 1973 (the very same year that Baron Rothschild was the head of the Union des Grand Crus).

[28] indicates that the region is best known for its white wines.

[29] the sweet white wines of Bordeaux's Sauternes region were also classified in 1855. Château d'Yquem was placed in a class of its own as a 'premier grand cru classé'.

[30] as a general rule: the more geographically-defined the provenance of a Burgundian wine, the higher its quality; 'grand cru' is the highest rank given to a vineyard followed by 'premier cru'.

[31] the mush of mainly dead yeast cells, bits of grape pulp, skins, stems and seeds that gravitates to the bottom of the barrel during fermentation. Wines that are deliberately left in contact with their lees acquire a specific flavour and complexity (such as the base wines that are later made into champagne).

[32] this is considered to be an up-and-coming wine region not only because its land is cheap and available for purchase by the so-called New World 'flying winemakers' (who are keen to experiment with a harvest in the

northern hemisphere) but also because some of its producers have chosen to reject regional winemaking practices in favour of experimentation. This has meant that their wines are officially classed outside the quality system and are only ranked as lowly 'Vins de Pays' (or Table wines) when they are actually vinified to a high quality and represent excellent value as everyday-drinking, fruity, New World-style wines.

[33] a wine business that is owned by a number of different (usually small) producers so that they may benefit from communal (and therefore cheaper) equipment and marketing costs as well as from EU subsidies.

[34] a type of wine merchant that buys either grapes, must or wines from smaller producers and blends them to sell under his own brand. Some also own their own vineyards. Négociants are more common in areas where vineyard holdings are small (such as Burgundy).

[35] the Napoleonic law of succession ruled that all possessions, including vineyards, had to be split equally amongst one's children.

[36] winemaking process that takes place prior to bottling which includes the addition of sulphur dioxide (to prevent unwanted microbiological changes) and a combination of refrigeration, filtration and fining to prevent subsequent chemical or physical changes occurring in the bottled wine such as unwanted deposits or haze.

[37] status in which new vintages or en primeur wines are first released by châteaux and under which duty charges can be deferred. This makes the trading and possible import and export of cases more straightforward. Once a wine has incurred duty it can no longer go back into bond.

[38] status of a wine once it has been taken out of bond and has incurred duty. Charges vary (they are usually lower in wine-producing countries than in non-wine producing countries) and may even be applied twice when exporting wines abroad (once on release, once upon arrival). Duty is either applied as a flat rate per litre (which is beneficial to consumers of expensive fine wines) or as a percentage of the wine's cost price.

[39] the method of buying wine futures traditionally only offered by the finest chateaux in Bordeaux in order to promote cash flow. Now increasingly offered by other small producers of fine wine in order to satisfy growing demand for en primeur investment opportunities.

[40] those distinguished by their fame and most notably price (which is often linked to a high score from the wine critic Robert Parker), even though this is not necessarily a reflection of their intrinsic quality but more a reflection

of their 'limited edition' status and of the strength of their marketing department.

[41] the space found in either a barrel or a bottle that is not occupied by wine. When referring to a barrel, ullage also means the process of evaporation that leads to that space; when referring to a bottle, the ullage is also known as the fill level. Ullage is a good indicator of past storage history especially when buying second-hand wines (such as at auction): the larger the space, the greater the risk of oxidation although it is important to bear the length of the cork in mind too (Château Mouton Rothschild now uses shorter-than-standard corks in order to reduce the amount of wine they absorb).

[42] innovative wines (produced in Italy since the 1970s) whose winemakers chose to ignore traditional wine regulations. As a result their wines qualified only for Table Wine status despite their quality and premium price.

[43] the connection of two halves of different vines by hand or machine so that they grow as one plant.

[44] musky: smelling and tasting like a wet, cheap fur coat.

[45] any type of non-vine plant that is deliberately cultivated between vine rows.

[46] a fungal disease which attacks the green parts of a vine (particularly young leaves).

[47] a particular way of pruning the vine that leaves only a certain number of canes to bud each year. Originally promoted by Dr Jules Guyot in the second half of the 19th Century, it is now also popular in the New World.

[48] commonly used in the vineyard (to feed the vine and prevent powdery mildew) as well as in the cellar both as a preservative (it prevents oxidation) and also as a killer of bacteria and wild yeasts which might impede a controlled fermentation and produce off flavours. The amount that can be added to wine is regulated because it can produce unpleasant aromas (the palate is quite sensitive to its presence, particularly in acidic white wines – too much sulphur and a wine can smell similar to one that is corked).

[49] this allows the winemaker to fine tune his grape must to exactly the style he requires (for example a Chardonnay must may be vinified to resemble a typical Sauvignon Blanc varietal and a Pinot Noir must can be vinified to display pronounced clove and nutmeg aromas). In the hands of more lazy, purely commercially-orientated producers however, the use of highly specific, flavour-inducing yeasts risks becoming yet another step in the potential homogenisation of the world's diverse wine styles.

## Acknowledgements

A huge thanks to the following people: to my parents for encouraging me to have an open mind, to question the status quo and to experiment with flavours and tastes from an early age; to my brother for his constructive criticism and for reading through so many proofs he can practically recite the book off by heart; to my boyfriend for the unfaltering support he provides; to Noel Young (of Noel Young Wines) for providing inspiration in the form of his amazing palate; to Jaspar Corbett (of Compass Wines) for the trust he put in me by sending me to Hong Kong to flap my wings, and finally to Tsun for waiting no less than four years for his birthday present (the reason I finally got round to completing this book)! Thanks also to Anthony Barne (Master of Wine) for fact-checking the content of the book and to Luke the designer for all his hard work in helping me to create my brand.

www.laviniabrown.co.uk